CW00686781

$\mathscr{T}$his book is a special gift

$\mathscr{T}$o:

Dr. Traci Langcake

$\mathscr{F}$rom:

Brian & Barbara Manners.

$\mathscr{D}$ate:

11 · 12 - 2003

$\mathscr{M}$essage:

Congratulations

Much love from us both.

Flowers of GOD'S GRACE

Catherine Marshall

Christian Art Gifts

FLOWERS OF GOD'S GRACE
by Catherine Marshall

Copyright © 1995 by Leonard LeSound
Originally published as an inspirational calendar under the title
Day by day with Catherine Marshall by Chosen Books, a
division of Baker Book House Company, Grand Rapids,
Michigan, 49516, USA.

Unless otherwise indicated, all Scripture quotations are taken
from the New American Standard Bible. Copyright © the Lockman
Foundation 1960, 1962, 1963, 1968, 1971, 1973, 1975, 1977.

© 2000 Christian Art, PO Box 1599,
Vereeniging, 1930, South Africa

Designed by Christian Art

ISBN 1-86852-597-X

Printed in Hong Kong

00 01 02 03 04 05 06 07 08 09 - 10 9 8 7 6 5 4 3 2 1

Flowers of
GOD'S
GRACE

JANUARY

JANUARY 1

GOD'S SOVEREIGNTY

"He knows the way I take;
when He has tried me, I
shall come forth as gold."
Job 23:10

Our God is the Divine Alchemist. He can take junk from the rubbish heap of life, and melting this base refuse in the pure fire of His love, hand us back – gold.

JANUARY 2

GOD'S SOVEREIGNTY

*"'Do I not fill the heavens and
the earth?' declares the Lord."*
Jeremiah 23:24

Like a great bell tolling over all the land,
the consistent voice of the sovereign power
of God reverberates throughout Old
Testament and New. He is omnipotent,
omnipresent, omniscient in this life and the
next. We cannot believe this and also think
that our God is no match for the evil of
the world.

JANUARY 3

GOD'S SOVEREIGNTY

*"I am like a luxuriant cypress;
from Me comes your fruit."*
Hosea 14:8

The Gospel truly is good news. The news is that there is no situation – no breakage, no loss, no grief, no sin, no mess – so dreadful that out of it God cannot bring good, total good, not just "spiritual" good, if we will allow Him to.

JANUARY 4

SURRENDER

*"And why do you call Me, 'Lord,
Lord,' and do not do what I say?"*
Luke 6:46

Any human physician requires the
surrender of a given case into his care; he
can do nothing unless the patient agrees
to follow his orders. Common sense told
me that exactly the same was true of the
Great Physician.

JANUARY 5

THE KINGDOM

"Seek first His kingdom and
His righteousness."
Matthew 6:33

"John is a great man, the greatest," Jesus was saying. "Yet the humblest disciple in the Kingdom has riches and privileges and authority of which John never dreamed." How could that be? Because man's efforts were at an end. In the new era of the Kingdom it would be God's Spirit *in* man doing the work.

JANUARY 6

ASKING

"Ask, and it shall be given to you."
Matthew 7:7

God insists that we ask, not because He needs to know our situation, but because *we* need the spiritual discipline of asking.

JANUARY 7

PRAYER

"For I, the Lord, do not change."
Malachi 3:6

The reason many of us retreat into vague generalities when we pray is not because we think too highly of God, but because we think too little.

PRAYER

*Jesus said to the centurion, "Go your way;
let it be done to you as you have believed."*
Matthew 8:13

In order to make sure that we are not retreating from the tension of faith, it is helpful to ask ourselves as we pray, "Do I really expect anything to happen?" This will prevent us from going window-shopping in prayer.

JANUARY 9

OUR WILL AND GOD'S

*... according to the kind
intention of His will.*
Ephesians 1:5

Because God loves us so much, He often guides us by planting His own lovely dream in the barren soil of a human heart. When the dream has matured, and the time for its fulfillment is ripe, to our astonishment and delight, we find that God's will has become our will, and our will, God's.

JANUARY 10

HUMOR

*"You blind guides, who strain
out a gnat and swallow a camel!"*
Matthew 23:24

Jesus' humor was always for a purpose. Sometimes it was His bridge to an individual He would otherwise have had trouble reaching. Most often it was to illuminate a truth.

JANUARY 11

HUMOR

"For it is easier for a camel to go through the eye of a needle, than for a rich man to enter the kingdom of God."
Luke 18:25

To awaken people at every level of their being, Jesus used every weapon of language and communication to achieve His goals; most effective were the humorous thrusts and banter about those who put on airs. Jesus sees all our incongruities and absurdities, and He laughs along with us.

JANUARY 12

GOD'S OMNISCIENCE

"Look at the birds of the air,
that they do not sow ... and yet
your heavenly Father feeds them. Are
you not worth much more than they?"
Matthew 6:26

Each of us is infinitely precious in the Father's sight, so much so that He knows every detail about us, even to the number of hairs on our heads.

JANUARY 13

Rewards

"And your reward will be great."
Luke 6:35

Jesus spoke often of heaven's rewards. If that offends us by seeming too materialistic, perhaps we should be wary of being more "spiritual" than our Lord.

JANUARY 14

LIFE AFTER DEATH

*"For in the resurrection they ...
are like angels in heaven."*
Matthew 22:30

I guessed that this meant that the one who has stepped over into the next life still remembers every tender moment on earth, still cares what happens to those left behind, still wants to help them – but that the emotion of his love is intensified and purified.

JANUARY 15

LIFE AFTER DEATH

Love never fails.
1 Corinthians 13:8

We have the apostle Paul, in his famous love poem, setting love at the summit of all spiritual gifts, describing for us in gladsome detail what it will be like someday. It was on this conception of a new kind of love, on a different kind of relationship that I had to fix my mind.

JANUARY 16

LIFE AFTER DEATH

When my anxious thoughts multiply within me, Thy consolations delight my soul.
Psalm 94:19

I remembered how often before Peter died that he had said from his pulpit, "Death has no scissors with which to cut the cords of love." Of course he had been right. Yet it is difficult for us to imagine love without possessiveness.

JANUARY 17

GUIDANCE

*We are the people of His pasture,
and the sheep of His hand.*
Psalm 95:7

Often God has to shut a door in our face
so that He can subsequently open the door
through which He wants us to go.

JANUARY 18

Answered Prayer

He will bring me out to the light,
and I will see His righteousness.
Micah 7:9

My Teacher had yet to show me the difference between the presumption that masquerades as faith and real faith. The dividing line between the two lies at the point of one's motive.

JANUARY 19

HEAVENLY FATHER

"How much more shall your heavenly Father give the Holy Spirit to those who ask Him?"
Luke 11:13

Jesus delighted in comparing earthly fathers to His heavenly Father, and then in adding, "But how much more God!" The riches of heaven and earth all belong to our Father, and He loves to shower them upon us. In Jesus' eyes, though, the most precious of all gifts is this one of the Holy Spirit.

JANUARY 20

GOD'S CARE

*"His father saw him ... and
ran and embraced him."*
Luke 15:20

God deals differently with each of us. He knows no "typical" case. He seeks us out at a point in our own need and runs down the road to meet us. This individualized treatment should delight rather than confuse us, because it so clearly reveals the highly personal quality of God's love and concern.

JANUARY 21

GOD'S CARE

*"And he who beholds Me
beholds the One who sent Me."*
John 12:45

Jesus' ringing response leaves no doubt: "I do choose. Be cleansed." And Jesus is the portrait of God. By every word and deed, Jesus made it clear that His Father not only cares, but that no detail of any life is too insignificant for His loving providence.

Joyfulness

(God) hath anointed Thee
with the oil of gladness.
Hebrews 1:9

As I read through the Gospels I see that Jesus had quite a bit to say about joy. We are not invited to a relationship that will take away our fun but asked to "enter into the joy of the Lord." The purpose of His coming to earth, Jesus said, was in order that our joy might be full!

JANUARY 23

JOYFULNESS

"In the world you have tribulation, but take courage; I have overcome the world."
John 16:33

I can see that Jesus drew men and women into the Kingdom by promising them two things: first trouble – hardship, danger; and second, joy. But what curious alchemy is this that He can make even danger and hardship seem joyous?

DAILY DEVOTIONS

*In the morning, O Lord, Thou
wilt hear my voice; in the
morning I will order my prayer
to Thee and eagerly watch.*
Psalm 5:3

It is wise to give God a chance to speak to us each day, perhaps the first thing in the morning when the mind is freshest. A few minutes of quietness help us focus on the areas where we most need God's help.

TRUST

*"And He gave Him authority ...
because He is the Son of Man."*
John 5:27

You are not really trusting God until you are trusting Him for the ultimates of life. And what are the ultimates? Life and death, health, economic necessities, the need to find one's own place in the world, to love and to be loved.

JANUARY 26

DOING FOR OURSELVES

*Not that we are adequate in ourselves
to consider anything as coming from
ourselves, but our adequacy is from God.*
2 Corinthians 3:5

I believe that the old cliché, "God helps those who help themselves," is not only misleading but often dead wrong. My most spectacular answers to prayers have come when I was so helpless, so out of control as to be able to do nothing at all for myself.

THE WORD

All things came into being
through Him; and apart from
Him nothing came into being
that has come into being.
John 1:3

Jesus stands sentinel over His Book to show us that we can use His word in Scripture with real power only as He Himself energizes it and speaks to us personally through it.

THE WORD

*How shall the ministry of the
Spirit fail to be even more with glory?*
2 Corinthians 3:8

Rhema is that part of the logos to which
the Holy Spirit points us personally, which
He illuminates and brings to life for us in
our particular situations.

JANUARY 29

PRAYERS

"For whoever wishes to save
his life shall lose it; but whoever
loses his life for My sake shall find it."
Matthew 16:25

God cannot get His word through to us when our prayers are limited to self-centered monologues.

JANUARY 30

BIBLE VERSES

(Jesus) entered the synagogue on the Sabbath, and stood up to read. And the book of the prophet Isaiah was handed to Him.
Luke 4:16-17

By saturating my mind with Bible verses I find that the grayness lifts, the spirit is infused with spiritual food and I am ready to meet any difficulty that comes along.

JANUARY 31

THE KING

"When He ascended on high,
He led captive a host of captives."
Ephesians 4:8

Until we catch a glimpse of the full glory of this crowned Christ, of the honors heaped upon Him, of the extent of the power the Father has placed in His hands, we can never grasp the significance of Jesus' question, "Who do you say that I am?" For Christ is the King of kings and the Lord of lords.

FEBRUARY

FEBRUARY 1

PRAISE

At that time Jesus answered and said, "I praise Thee, O Father, Lord of heaven and earth."
Matthew 11:25

My first discovery was that I knew almost nothing about praise. The subject is mentioned occasionally as a nice worship exercise, a sort of icing on the cake as a gesture to God, but praise as the key to answered prayer, no. That was a new concept altogether.

Praise

*Yet Thou art holy, O Thou who art
enthroned upon the praises of Israel.*
Psalm 22:3

The quickest way to go to meet Him is through praise. No wonder we meet Him there, for Scripture goes on to teach us that God actually "inhabits" (lives in) the praises of His people.

Praise

*Through Him then, let us continually
offer up a sacrifice of praise to God.*
Hebrews 13:15

The fact that the word "sacrifice" is used regarding praise tells us that the writers of Scripture understood well that when we praise God for trouble, we're giving up something. What we're sacrificing is the right to the blessings we think are due to us.

FEBRUARY 4

PRAISE

Thou art my God, and I give thanks to Thee.
Psalm 118:28

Even as God asked praise of Jehoshaphat and of Paul and Silas, so He asks it of each one of us. And the longer one ponders this matter of praise and experiments with it, the more evidence comes to light that here is the most powerful prayer of all, a golden bridge to the heart of God.

FEBRUARY 5

PRAISE

*The cords of the wicked have encircled me,
But I have not forgotten Thy law. At midnight I shall rise to give thanks to Thee ...*
Psalm 119:61-62

We must begin to praise by obeying Jesus' injunction "Resist not evil." So we stop fighting whatever form evil is at the moment taking.

Praise

*For Thy righteousness, O God, reaches
to the heavens, Thou who hast done
great things; O God, who is like Thee?
Psalm 71:19*

Praise is the swiftest, surest route to faith.

FEBRUARY 7

Soul Searching

*And everyone who has this
hope fixed on Him purifies
himself, just as He is pure.*
1 John 3:3

He is always Light, so I too must walk in
the light. All closed doors, every shuttered
room in me must be thrown open. So began
months of soul searching.

FEBRUARY 8

THE BIBLE

Thy word is a lamp to my feet.
Psalm 119:105

I wanted authoritative answers. Therefore, I went directly to the most authoritative source I knew – the Scriptures. And I discovered what I should have known before – that when you and I go to the Bible out of great need to learn what it has to say to us, it is then that we get real help.

FEBRUARY 9

PRAYER

Worship the Lord with reverence,
and rejoice with trembling.
Psalm 2:11

God, who created heaven and earth, will hear *my* voice? The King of the universe will consider *my* meditation? Oh, thank You, Lord, for the undreamed-of opportunity of this audience with the King!

FAITH

*Now faith is ... the conviction
of things not seen.*
Hebrews 11:1

Faith is not hocus-pocus, opposed to knowledge and reality. In fact, faith does not go against experience at all; rather it appeals to experience, just as science does. The difference is that it appeals to experience in a realm where our five senses are not supreme rulers.

FAITH

*By faith Abraham, when he was called,
obeyed by going out to a place which he
was to receive for an inheritance; and he
went out, not knowing where he was going.*
Hebrews 11:8

Faith in God is simply trusting Him
enough to step out on that trust.

Faith

By faith Moses, when he was born, was hidden for three months by his parents, because they saw he was a beautiful child; and they were not afraid of the king's edict.
Hebrews 11:23

Faith is strengthened only as we ourselves exercise it. We have to apply it to our problems: poverty, bodily ills, bereavement, job troubles, tangled human relationships.

Faith

*"To give to His people the knowledge of
salvation by the forgiveness of their sins,
because of the tender mercy of our God ..."*
Luke 1:77-78

We cannot have faith and a guilty con-
science at the same time. Every time faith
will fade away.

Faith

> *"Blessed is she who believed that there would be a fulfillment of what had been spoken to her by the Lord."*
> Luke 1:43-45

Faith has to be in the present tense – now. A vague prospect that what we want will transpire in the future is not faith, but hope.

Faith

The Lord is our lawgiver, the
Lord is our king; He will save us.
Isaiah 33:22

Faith means that we must let Him do the work. Almost always it takes longer than we think it should. When we grow impatient and try a deliverance of our own, through friends or circumstances, we are taking God's work out of His hands.

Faith

"Do you believe that I am able to do this?"
Matthew 9:28

Once I thought that faith was believing this or that specific thing in my mind with never a doubt. Now I know that faith is nothing more or less than actively trusting God.

FEBRUARY 17

A Purpose

And the Lord said to him, "Arise
and go to the street called Straight."
Acts 9:11

The idea that He might have a particular
purpose for any one of us – a reason why
we are here on earth – boggles the mind.
So as He begins to unfold that bigger
design into which we fit, it is up to us to
take the first step forward in obedience.

FREE IN CHRIST

*But know that the Lord has
set apart the godly man for Himself;
the Lord hears when I call to Him.*
Psalm 4:3

The psalmist says that when he is hemmed in on every side, the Lord frees him. Gradually I have learned to recognize this hemming-in as one of God's most loving devices for teaching us that He is real and gloriously adequate for our problems.

OBEDIENCE

As a result of the works, faith was perfected.
James 2:22

Nor can trust ever end in just intellectual faith or lip service to faith. When it is the real thing, it will spill over into action — and that will mean obedience.

OBEDIENCE

*For it is God who is at work in you, both
to will and to work for His good pleasure.*
Philippians 2:13

How can we *not* want to obey when we
begin to comprehend the magnitude of the
Holy Spirit's love and complete good will
for us?

FEBRUARY 21

IMPURITIES

Let us keep living by that same
standard to which we have attained.
Philippians 3:16

I knew that anything unloving in me, any resentment, unforgiveness or impurity would shut out God, just as a muddy windowpane obscures the sunlight.

CONVICTION

And he said, "Who art Thou, Lord?" And He said, "I am Jesus whom you are persecuting."
Acts 9:5

Here we have Jesus telling us that convicting one another is not, and never was, our work: It's the Holy Spirit's business. Each of us must receive illumination about his guilt from the inside.

FEBRUARY 23

FORGIVENESS

And if he has committed sins,
they will be forgiven him.
James 5:15

Long ago we had learned the principle that it is necessary to get the past confessed and straightened out (as far as is possible) before we can live abundantly in the present.

FEBRUARY 24

FORGIVENESS

*For Thou, Lord, art good, and ready
to forgive, and abundant in loving-
kindness to all who call upon Thee.*
Psalm 86:5

Forgiveness is the precondition of love.

WEALTH

*The earth is the Lord's,
and all it contains.*
Psalm 24:1

If I truly believe that I am a child of a King, then my fear will disappear. Worrying would be the sure sign that I did not believe God's ownership of earth's resources. To think myself a pauper is to deny either the King's riches or my being His beloved child.

FAMILIES

"Just as the Father has loved me, I have also loved you; abide in My love."
John 15:9

There's no way to get our world back together again except as each of us begins with himself and with his own family.

Fear

*The Lord is the defense of my
life; whom shall I dread?*
Psalm 27:1

Fear is like a screen erected between us and God so that His power cannot get through to us.

FEAR

Thou hast removed all the wicked of the earth like dross; therefore I love Thy testimonies.
Psalm 119:119

Sometimes it helps to write down one's fears, then hold them up one by one to the light of Christ's clear understanding. Never is Jesus as the Light of the world more clear than in these murky areas of our semiconscious fears, most of them unreal and psychotic.

FEAR

*"Why are you troubled, and why
do doubts arise in your hearts?"*
Luke 24:38

The time came when I realized that, in Jesus' eyes, fear is a sin since it is acting out a lack of trust in God.

MARCH

MARCH 1

FEAR

"And there is no other God besides Me, a righteous God and a Savior; there is none except Me."
Isaiah 45:21

Faith is the strong tower into which we can run for protection today. It isn't a physical place but the light of a protecting Presence. It makes the unreal fears vanish and gives us literal protection against the real ones.

MARCH 2

HELPLESSNESS

What then shall we say to these things?
If God is for us, who is against us?
Romans 8:31

Sometimes life finds us powerless before facts that cannot be changed. Then we can only stand still at the bottom of the pit and claim for our particular trouble that best of all promises, that God will make even this to "work together for good."

HELPLESSNESS

*"For the Lord God is my strength and song,
and He has become my salvation."*
Isaiah 12:2

Why would God insist on helplessness as a prerequisite to answered prayer? One obvious reason is because our human helplessness is bedrock fact. God is a realist and insists that we be realists too.

MARCH 4

HELPLESSNESS

"Call to Me, and I will answer you,
and I will tell you great and mighty
things, which you do not know."
Jeremiah 33:3

It should not surprise us that creativity arises out of the pit of life rather than the high places. For creativity is the ability to put old material into new form. And it is only when old molds are broken up by need or suffering, compelling us to regroup, that the creative process starts to flow.

Inherited Traits

So rejoice, O sons of Zion,
And be glad in the Lord your God.
Joel 2:23

Just as we can inherit either a fortune or debts, so in the spiritual realm we can inherit either spiritual blessings or those liabilities (unabashedly called "sins" in Scripture) that hinder our development into mature persons.

MARCH 6

GIVING

*"There is a lad here, who has
five barley loaves, and two fish, but
what are these for so many people?"
Jesus said, "Have the people sit down."*
John 6:9-10

The secret of receiving is to give – even
out of poverty. In fact, the more sunk we
are in visions of lack, the greater need we
have to start giving.

MARCH 7

IMMORTALITY

He heals the brokenhearted ...
Psalm 147:3

My first discovery was that reading what the Bible has to say about death and immortality immediately bathes the subject in the sunlight of normalcy. What a grave injustice we do ourselves when we fail to take advantage of this help and go on through life fearing and wondering!

IMMORTALITY

For now we see in a mirror
dimly, but then face to face.
1 Corinthians 13:13

The New Testament reassures us that the next life is not only a fully conscious one with every intellectual and spiritual faculty intact, but that these faculties are heightened.

MARCH 9

IMMORTALITY

"In my Father's house are many dwelling places; if it were not so, I would have told you."
John 14:2

We shall be able to remember, to think, to will, to love, to worship and to understand so much more on the other side of the barrier of death. Our new life will be no sleeping, non-conscious or unfeeling existence.

MARCH 10

IMMORTALITY

*"Truly I say to you, today you
shall be with Me in Paradise."*
Luke 23:43

Christ's words to the dying thief would
have been nonsense had He not meant that
after death on that very day, both He and
the thief would know themselves to be
themselves, would remember that they had
suffered together, would recognize each
other.

MARCH 11

THE SUBCONSCIOUS

For all who are being led by the
Spirit of God, these are sons of God.
Romans 8:14

The Christian may be permitted to wonder whether somewhere in the deeps of personality – still beyond the reach of our scientific probing and measuring – there is not a place where the Spirit that is God can impress upon the spirit that is man a thought, a direction, a solution.

BORN OF THE SPIRIT

*"This is the one who
baptizes in the Holy Spirit."*
John 1:33

Scripture makes it clear that Jesus Himself
is the only One who can baptize us with
the Spirit. That is why there must always
be the first step of commitment to Jesus
(being "born again") before we can receive
the fullness of His Spirit.

THE BATTLE

"Do not resist him who is evil."
Matthew 5:39

The way to win out when I feel evil at work in my life and the lives of those I love is not to fight it in the ordinary sense, but to give over those I love completely into the Father's hands, knowing that I am helpless to cope with evil, but that He is able.

MARCH 14

ILLNESS

The Lord is my shepherd.
Psalm 23:1

The unforgettable truth of David's Psalm 23 came alive in my experience: "He *maketh* me to lie down in green pastures" – thus sometimes using illness to get our full attention.

MARCH 15

HUMAN RESOURCES

Examine yourselves!
2 Corinthians 13:5

So long as we are deluding ourselves that human resources can supply our heart's desires, we are believing a lie. And it is impossible for prayers to be answered out of a foundation of self-deception and untruth.

MARCH 16

REDEMPTION

*In Him you have been made complete, and He
is the head over all rule and authority.*
Colossians 2:10

God is not going to drop into our laps, as
a package commodity, unselfishness or a
loving disposition or any virtue. Instead,
He has promised me Jesus' resurrection life
in me. Thus it will be Jesus' selflessness
and patience and love manifested in my
life – not my own.

FAITHFULNESS

Great is Thy faithfulness.
Lamentations 3:23

Reading through the journals of my college years makes me aware as never before how tender God was with me, never intruding on my willful self-centeredness, but always there when the heart hungers inside me cried out.

DIVIDENDS

*"For even the Son of Man did
not come to be served, but to serve."*
Mark 10:45

Jesus told His disciples to tarry until they received the Holy Spirit's power to become His witnesses. Note that Jesus did not say that this gift is for our own spiritual development or perfection or happiness. All of those results will follow provided we accept Jesus' top priority – witnessing to the world.

MARCH 19

GUIDANCE

"O Lord, be Thou my helper."
Psalm 30:10

Apparently the surrender of self is necessary groundwork for receiving guidance, since not even God can lead us until we want to be led. It is as if we are given an inner receiving set at birth, but the set is not tuned in until we actively turn our lives over to God.

GUIDANCE

*"For where your treasure is,
there will your heart be also."*
Matthew 6:21

Most of us think of our lives in compartments – home life, business life, social life. Actually the various aspects of a truly creative life must dovetail. God will not direct a man's business life, for example, when the man insists on running his family life his own way.

GUIDANCE

Commit your works to the Lord,
and your plans will be established.
Proverbs 16:3

In seeking guidance, I discovered that it was important to concentrate on one or two questions on which I needed light, and ask God for directions on those. This selectivity proved more effective than trying to make my mind blank, ready to receive any message on any subject.

MARCH 22

GUIDANCE

These all with one mind were continually
devoting themselves to prayer.
Acts 1:14

One reason the first Christians received so much guidance was that they had *koinonia*, a corporate fellowship that made them "of one heart and soul." It was in this setting that illumination, inspiration and guidance flourished.

GUIDANCE

"He who is holy, who is true,
... who opens and no one will shut,
and who shuts and no one opens."
Revelation 3:7

Then there is the check of providential circumstances. We are most fortunate in having this test. When we have asked God to guide us, we have to accept by faith the fact that He is doing so. This means that when He closes a door in our faces, we do well not to try to crash that door.

Guidance

*The mind of a man plans his
way, but the Lord directs his steps.*
Proverbs 16:9

I found in the matter of guidance that I had to be willing to obey – no matter what. Otherwise no directions would be forthcoming. Receiving guidance is definitely not a matter of telling God what we want and hoping that He will approve.

MARCH 25

GUIDANCE

*"Sanctify them in the truth;
Thy word is truth."*
John 17:17

I have found that the inner Voice is more likely to speak to me at the first moment of consciousness upon awakening, or during some odd moment of the day as I go about routine tasks, than while I wait expectantly with pad and pencil in hand.

MARCH 26

GIFTS

*Pursue love, yet desire
earnestly spiritual gifts.*
1 Corinthians 14:1

So far as the virtues and graces we need
for victory in our lives – faith, joy, patience,
peace of mind, the ability to love the
wretched and the unlovely – there is no
way we can work up such qualities. Paul
tells us that these are gifts of the Holy Spirit.
They can be had in no other way.

Ministry

*Whoever wishes to become great
among you shall be your servant.*
Mark 10:43

Are we ready to give ourselves to others? He will accept no excuses about our inadequacy in this way or that. Giving us adequacy is His business. That's what His coming to us is all about.

FREE WILL

*And He said to them, "What
do you want Me to do for you?"*
Mark 10:36

Jesus had told me what to do. At that
moment I understood as never before the
totality of His respect for the free will He
has given us and the fact that He will *never*
violate it. His attitude said, "The decision
is entirely yours."

MARCH 29

SELF-SUFFICIENCY

For by grace you have been saved through
faith; and ... not as a result of works.
Ephesians 2:8-9

We want salvation from our sins and we yearn for eternal life. We think that we can earn these things. Then we find out, as Paul did, that we cannot pile up enough good marks and merits to earn anything from God. No, salvation "is the gift of God; not as a result of works, that no one should boast."

MARCH 30

OUT OF CONTROL

"Apart from me you can do nothing."
John 15:5

Sometime in life every one of us finds himself out of control, caught in circumstances that he is helpless to change. We are to welcome such times. Often it is only then that we lesser spirits enter into the truth of Jesus' statement from the fifteenth chapter of John: "Apart from Me you can do nothing."

SEEKING APPROVAL

For they loved the approval of men
rather than the approval of God.
John 12:43

Certainly there is enormous pressure on all of us to be accepted and approved by others. But God wants us to resist this pressure. Consider the tragedy of the religious leaders of Jesus' day.

APRIL

APRIL 1

TWO WINGS

Be renewed in the spirit of your mind.
Ephesians 4:23

In order to fly we must have two wings. One wing is the realization of our human helplessness, the other is the realization of God's power. Our faith in God's ability to handle our particular situation is the connecting link.

APRIL 2

Fellowship With Christ

"Abide in Me, and I in you."
John 15:4

Fellowship with Jesus is the true purpose of life and the only foundation for eternity. It is real, this daily fellowship He offers us.

APRIL 3

HOPE

I will wait for the Lord ... I
will even look eagerly for Him.
Isaiah 8:17

For each of us — no matter what our situation or how we feel we have failed — there is hope.

APRIL 4

EXHIBITIONISM

*There will be silence before Thee,
and praise in Zion, O God ...*
Psalm 65:1

Scripture makes it clear that the Holy Spirit is not fond of exhibitionism. After all, no trumpets herald the pinky-gray opalescent dawn. No bugles announce the opening of a rosebud. God speaks not in the thunder or the roaring wind, rather in a "still, small voice."

APRIL 5

SOVEREIGNTY

"Do you think that I cannot appeal to My Father, and He will at once put at My disposal more than twelve legions of angels?"
Matthew 26:53

It would seem to us that if ever the free will of wicked men was in control, it was at the execution of Jesus Christ by crucifixion. "Not so," was Jesus' assertion. Never for an instant during the acting out of that drama did God abdicate as sovereign ruler.

PLEASING GOD

Whatever you do, do your work heartily,
as for the Lord rather than for men.
Colossians 3:23

We are told that in our daily task –
whatever our vocation or profession or daily
round – we are to seek to please God more
than man.

Material Needs

*Your heavenly Father knows
that you need all these things.*
Matthew 6:32

As for whether God means for us to include material needs in our petitions, certainly Christ was interested in men's bodies as well as their souls. He was concerned about their diseases, their physical hunger. Christianity, almost alone among world religions, acknowledges material things as real and important.

APRIL 8

OBEDIENCE

"Thy will be done, on earth as it is in heaven."
Matthew 6:10

God does not want our obedience out of fear. Our obedience to Him is the fruit of lives growing in the rich soil of love and trust. Our obedience is to be at once both the result of our loving God and also the proof of our love.

APRIL 9

OBEDIENCE

*"I did not come to abolish
(the Law), but to fulfill (it)."*
Matthew 5:17

But what exactly are we to obey? Since
Jesus often mentioned His commandments,
I found it helpful to read the Gospels
through, setting down in a notebook the
commandments that Christ Himself gave
us. There are a remarkable number of them
and many are surprisingly precise.

APRIL 10

OBEDIENCE

*And when they saw Him,
they worshiped Him.*
Matthew 28:17

Not one of us is going to drop his fishing nets, leave all and go after Jesus – unless he feels he can trust Him. One memorable sentence quoted by Quakeress Hannah Smith sums it up: "Perfect obedience would be perfect happiness if only we had perfect confidence in the power we were obeying."

APRIL 11

OBEDIENCE

"Incline your ear and come to Me."
Isaiah 55:3

Always and always the understanding comes after the obedience.

OBEDIENCE

For by it (faith) the men
of old gained approval.
Hebrews 11:2

So Abraham obeyed. "He went out, not knowing whither he went." He did not need to know because God knew.

THE LEADING OF THE SPIRIT

"When He, the Spirit of truth, comes,
He will guide you into all the truth."
John 16:13

Sometimes even as I would open my mouth to speak, there would be a sharp check on the inside. I soon learned that the Holy Spirit sought to prevent careless words or critical words or even too many words. Nor would He tolerate even a trace of sarcasm, or faithless words of doubt or fear.

Judging Others

*"For in the way you judge,
you will be judged."*
Matthew 7:2

Jesus was simply stating a law of life when He told us, "Judge and you will be judged." Put this way, judging others constantly cultivates more soil for the thistles of fear-of-man to grow in.

APRIL 15

CONCENTRATION

*And their eyes were opened
and they recognized Him.*
Luke 24:31

God asks that we worship Him with concentrated minds as well as allowing the Spirit to direct our wills and emotions. A divided and scattered mind is not at its most receptive.

LOVE

*"And you shall love the Lord your
God with all your heart and with
all your soul and with all your might."*
Deuteronomy 6:5

We are going to be capable of loving only
to the extent that we abandon ourselves to
another with no reservations.

Prayer

"Listen to me, you who ... seek the Lord: Look to the rock from which you were hewn."
Isaiah 51:1

Praying requires patience. God's perfect timing oftener than not seems slow – slow – slow to us.

APRIL 18

LISTENING

*"And I will make all My mountains a
road, and My highways will be raised up."*
Isaiah 49:11

I found that in the everydayness of life
when the inner guidance did not obviously
violate any of God's loving laws or hurt
another, it was important to obey and thus
experiment with obedience. That was how
I learned to recognize the Holy Spirit's
voice.

APRIL 19

The Next Life

*Then I shall know fully just
as I also have been fully known.*
1 Corinthians 13:12

Scripture piles reassurance upon reassurance that at the death of the physical body, the real person inside lives on without interruption. The Bible tells us that the next life is not only a fully conscious one with every intellectual and spiritual faculty intact but that these faculties are heightened.

THE NEXT LIFE

*May Thy compassion come
to me that I may live.*
Psalm 119:77

When we become aware of damaged areas in the unconscious, we can call on the power of the Holy Spirit. He can walk back with us into the past, drain out all the poison, then create a highway for our God to come marching triumphantly into the present with His long-forgotten, oft-delayed plan for our lives.

JESUS' VOICE

"My sheep hear My voice, and I know them, and they follow Me."
John 10:27

It is when we try to hear Christ's voice for the daily decisions that we begin to know Jesus personally. Most people are astonished at His interest in the details of this relationship: how well He knows us, all the little things we thought we had successfully hidden.

Protection

God is to us a God of deliverance.
Psalm 68:20

If we were willing to accept the Spirit's help and to listen to His voice, many of the evils, difficulties and accidents that befall us would be avoided. I believe this to be an important answer to the question so often asked, "How could a loving God allow such-and-such a dreadful calamity to happen?"

TRUSTING GOD

*Blessed be the Lord, who
daily bears our burden.*
Psalm 68:19

So if your every human plan and calculation has miscarried, if, one by one, human props have been knocked out, and doors have shut in your face, take heart. God is trying to get a message through to you, and the message is: "Stop depending on inadequate human resources. Let Me handle the matter."

APRIL 24

FAITH

*"And all things you ask in prayer,
believing, you shall receive."*
Matthew 21:22

In one of the greatest blank-check promises Jesus left us, He pinned everything to faith.

Faith

*Now faith is the assurance
of things hoped for ...*
Hebrews 11:1

Faith always has to be in the present
(denoting completed action), as contrasted
with hope, which is always in the future.

FAITH

*Commit your way to the Lord, trust
also in Him, and He will do it.*
Psalm 37:5

There is much in Scripture stressing our
need to have faith in God. Psalm 37:5
takes us a step further. It not only admon-
ishes us to trust, it promises that when we
do, God will act in a supernatural way to
answer our need. Dwell on that for a
moment. We trust, God acts.

APRIL 27

Faith

*For with Thee is the fountain
of life; in Thy light we see light.*
Psalm 36:9

Clearly it was Jesus' desire that we be rid
of disease. What was His plan for achieving
this? He said that faith in His Father's willingness and ability to give His children all
good gifts is the key. In His eyes there was
no evil that faith could not vanquish, no
need that faith could not supply.

SUPERSPIRITUALITY

*And He was teaching them
many things in parables.*
Mark 4:2

Substituting a type of superspirituality for
Jesus' homespun practicality can be one
subtle way many of us try to keep a safe
distance between Him and us.

Human Need

*And in the same way the Spirit
also helps us in our weakness; for we
do not know how to pray as we should.*
Romans 8:26

Actually, when we human beings feel most capable of handling life on our own, invariably that is when we are most in need of Jesus' help mediated to us by the Spirit.

ABIDING

"He who abides in Me, and I
in him, he bears much fruit."
John 15:5

Our human hang-up is thinking that spirituality is something we do. "Not so," says Jesus. "Rather it is My life in you." The branch's part is simply to remain connected to the Vine, to abide there so that the lifegiving sap can flow.

MAY

DREAMS

Then the mystery was revealed
to Daniel in a night vision.
Daniel 2:19

The unconscious mind does not think analytically, but symbolically or pictorially. Dream symbols are provocative in their wide variety and above all in their originality.

DREAMS

*"This mystery has ... been
revealed to me ... that you may
understand the thoughts of your mind."*
Daniel 2:30

Our dreams are often intensely personal and self-reflective. Something deep within seeks to give us a message. Different characters in our dreams are usually parts of our own being. Aspects of our personality that we have ignored or even cast out of our consciousness now seek to be heard.

ALL-OUT TRUST

*Though the yield of the olive should
fail, and the fields produce no food,
... yet I will exult in the Lord.*
Habakkuk 3:17-18

There are periods when God's face is
shrouded, when His dealings with us will
appear as if He does not care, when He
seems not to be acting like a true Father.
Can we then hang onto the fact of His love
and His faithfulness and that He *is* a
prayer-answering God?

MAY 4

ALL-OUT TRUST

When my anxious thoughts multiply within me, Thy consolations delight my soul.
Psalm 94:19

Can we, *at the moment* when His face is hidden, exult in the God of our salvation?

MAY 5

THE FAMILY

*Today, if you would hear His
voice, do not harden your hearts.*
Psalm 95:7-8

Consider Jesus' admonition that we
forgive seventy times seven. Perhaps Christ
was not thinking specifically of the family
unit when He spoke those words, or I think
He might have trebled the figure.

THE FAMILY

*Fathers, do not provoke your children
to anger; but bring them up in the
discipline and instruction of the Lord.*
Ephesians 6:4

The family is meant to be the training
ground for life, a true microcosm for the
world outside the home where person has
to get along with person, pupils with each
other and with teachers, employees with
bosses, management with labor, nation
with nation.

THE FAMILY

As many as received Him,
to them He gave the right
to become children of God.
John 1:12

The master design for us to advance toward our heavenly home via the nitty-gritty of family life would be just like Him.

MAY 8

CLEANSING

*And He (Jesus) stretched out His
hand and touched him, saying,
"I am willing; be cleansed."*
Matthew 8:3

Jesus healed because the love of God
flowing irresistibly through Him in a
torrent of good will simply swept evil away
as the debris that it is.

MAY 9

THE CROSS

"Not what I will, but what Thou wilt."
Mark 14:36

In the Garden of Gethsemane Jesus deliberately set himself to make His will and God's will the same. God has given you and me free will too. And the voluntary giving up of our self-will has a cross at the center of it.

THE CROSS

*(Let us fix) ... our eyes on Jesus, the
author and perfecter of faith, who for
the joy set before Him endured the cross,
despising the shame, and has sat down
at the right hand of the throne of God.*
Hebrews 12:2

The crucifixion and resurrection are
history's watershed.

MAY 11

THE CROSS

*"Repent, and let each of you be
baptized in the name of Jesus Christ
for the forgiveness of your sins."*
Acts 2:38

With the cross, God wiped out the old
creation that was flawed in Eden. The
Gospel's momentous news is not only that
Jesus died on that cross, but that you and
I and our flawed natures also died with
Him.

MAY 12

THE CROSS

*Even when we were dead in our transgres-
sions, (God) made us alive together with
Christ ... and raised us up with Him ...*
Ephesians 2:5-6

Not only that, even as I was "in" Christ
on His Cross, so I also rose with Him, have
been set in the heavenlies with Him, and
I am now complete only in Him.

THE CROSS

*(God) seated us with Him ... in
order that in the ages to come He
might show the surpassing riches of His
grace in kindness toward us in Christ Jesus.*
Ephesians 2:6-7

Ever afterward there would be men and
women who would glory in that cross
"towering o'er the wrecks of time" – the
wrecks that we always manage to make
in every century. They would glory because
the cross stands as the final symbol that
no evil exists that God cannot turn into a
blessing.

THE HEART'S DESIRE

*Neither has the eye seen a
God besides Thee, who acts in
behalf of the one who waits for Him.*
Isaiah 64:4

God has a "fullness of time" for the answer to each of our prayers. It follows then, that He alone knows the magnitude of the changes that have to be wrought in us before we can receive our heart's desires.

THE HEART'S DESIRE

*Let us not lose heart in doing good, for in due
time we shall reap if we do not grow weary.*
Galatians 6:9

God alone knows the changes and
interplay of external events that must take
place before our prayers can be answered.

MADE PERFECT

(The body) is raised in glory ...
it is raised in power.
1 Corinthians 15:43

The Scriptures say that we shall have a spiritual body after death. This spiritual body will give us much the same appearance that we have had on earth, except that if imperfect or deformed or diseased, all will be made perfect.

THE RESURRECTION

*"See My hands and My feet, that
it is I Myself; touch Me and see."*
Luke 24:39

Those who speak of some sort of "spiritual resurrection" are missing the point. Nothing short of the resurrection of the flesh would have been any victory at all. Satan would not have been deceived; Jesus' surprised, incredulous disciples would not, and neither would we.

Faith Vs. Fear

"In the world you have tribulation, but take courage; I have overcome the world."
John 16:33

Faith is always right; fear and despair are always wrong.

VICTORY

*"All things have been handed
over to Me by My Father."*
Luke 10:22

When Christ's apostles returned, after having healed successfully, He rejoiced with them, "I watched Satan falling from heaven like a flash of lightning." As restrained as the narrative usually is, a lilting, triumphant quality breaks through here. Luke says that Jesus "rejoiced greatly" at that hour.

VICTORY

*"Take My yoke upon you,
and learn from Me."*
Matthew 11:29

We can allow an apparent defeat to turn into victory through trusting in the principle of resurrection. As Easter was not a passive event, neither is this kind of waiting. Here, too, something must be put to death, usually worry or trying to do it yourself.

GRIEF

He has sent me to bind
up the brokenhearted.
Isaiah 61:1

The Bible does not ignore sorrow as a fact of human experience. Some of the loveliest words of Scripture are for the sore of heart.

ABSTRACTIONS

*"If God so arrays the grass of
the field ... will He not much more
do so for you, O men of little faith?"*
Matthew 6:30

Most of us are not anything like as realistic
as our God. We like to deal with high-
flown theological abstractions. He deals
with the lilies of the field, the yeast in the
housewife's bread, patches on garments.

DECISION

"No one can serve two masters."
Matthew 6:24

It is as if nothing had changed since that moment eons ago when man was presented with his stark choice: Would he believe God or Satan? Time is still holding its breath for our answer. Which way will each man, each woman, decide now?

MAY 24

HEALING

He said, "It is not those who are healthy who need a physician, but those who are ill."
Matthew 9:12

Jesus came to earth to show us the Father's will. He who created the incredible human body still heals today, but not as a divine magician. We need to seek His way, His timing and the lessons He wants us to learn along the way.

HEALING

*(Jesus) ... healed all who were ill in order that
what was spoken through Isaiah the prophet
might be fulfilled, saying, "He Himself took our
infirmities, and carried away our diseases."*
Matthew 8:16-17

Healing is not an end in itself; it is a
dividend of the Gospel.

HEALING

And when the Lord saw her,
He felt compassion for her.
Luke 7:13

Jesus' chief motive in healing seems to have been nothing more or less than pure compassion. The word *compassion* is used over and over to describe His attitude toward the sick. That was why He often went out of His way to heal when the sufferer had neither asked for nor thought of His doing so.

HEALING

*She was saying to herself, "If I only
touch His garment, I shall get well."*
Matthew 9:21

Practically speaking, we shall have taken
our greatest step forward in the realm of
spiritual healing when the average
Christian becomes as sure of God's will for
health as he is of his doctor's. Only those
who have settled this in their own minds,
can press forward in the adventure of spiritual research.

HEALING

*And all the multitude were trying
to touch Him, for power was coming
from Him and healing them all.*
Luke 6:19

He (Jesus) did not once say in regard to
health, "If it is God's will."

Healing

And He touched her hand,
and the fever left her.
Matthew 8:15

There is no beatitude for the sick as there is for others like the bereaved of those who suffer persecution. Nor did there ever fall from Jesus' lips any statements that ill health would further our spiritual growth or benefit the Kingdom. Rather, He not only wants to heal our diseases, He also wants us to stay healthy.

HEALING

*Jesus said to Him, "Arise, take
up your pallet, and walk."*
John 5:8

Jesus healed out of pure compassion
because He was ever "The Father's
Restorer." True, after Jesus healed the man
at the Pool of Bethesda, He told him that
now he would be wise to repent and change
lest something even worse happen. But the
healing came before the man's change and
in no way seemed dependent on it.

THE GIVER

*The man believed the word
that Jesus spoke to him.*
John 4:50

I've learned that our Lord waits patiently until we stop playing games with Him. The instant we leave off our childish fooling around, He knows it and responds. It had taken me eighteen months of trying everything else, but at last I wanted the Giver more than His gifts.

JUNE

JUNE 1

FULFILLMENT

*And we know that God causes all things to
work together for good to those who love God.*
Romans 8:28

True praise grows out of the recognition
and acknowledgement that in His time
God will bring good out of bad. There is
the intolerable situation on the one hand
and the fulfillment of Romans 8:28 on the
other hand.

JUNE 2

SEPARATION

For I am convinced that neither death,
nor life ... nor any other created thing,
shall be able to separate us from the love
of God, which is in Christ Jesus our Lord.
Romans 8:38-39

Nothing can separate us from His love except our own blind unwillingness to receive.

JUNE 3

REVELATION

For if we died with Him,
we shall also live with Him.
2 Timothy 2:11

Surely there is no joy like that first rush of discovery in experiencing for oneself that the Lord is alive in one's life. And I had stumbled into that revelation in the last way I would have thought logical – through the relinquishment of myself to Him.

PRAYER LOG

A book of remembrance was written before Him.
Malachi 3:16

If we hadn't been recording both the prayer requests and the answers with dates, we might have assumed these to be "coincidences." With those written notations marking the answers to prayer, we found our gratitude to God mounting. The prayer log was a marvelous stimulus to faith.

ANSWERS TO PRAYER

*And He did not do many miracles
there because of their unbelief.*
Matthew 13:58

Gradually I saw that a demanding spirit,
with self-will as its rudder, blocks prayer. I
understood that the reason for this is that
God absolutely refuses to violate our free
will; that, therefore, unless self-will is
voluntarily given up, even God cannot
move to answer prayer.

JUNE 6

FOLLOWING HIS LEAD

He leads me beside quiet waters.
Psalm 23:2

My problem was that often I was not content to have the Good Shepherd lead me into truth. Like a rambunctious sheep, I kept running on ahead, nosing around the pasture-land, always thinking that the truth I sought must surely lie immediately on the other side of the nearest hill.

JUNE 7

JESUS' WILL

"Now I am going to Him who sent Me."
John 16:5

Since Jesus' perfect humanity was as real as His divinity, His would have been a strong human will, stronger than any of ours. Over and over He reiterated that He had handed over that will.

JUNE 8

JESUS' WILL

And a voice came out of heaven, "Thou art My beloved Son, in Thee I am well-pleased."
Luke 3:22

Reading between the lines of the Gospel records, I believe that Jesus relinquished His will each time He desired to heal a sufferer, then immediately looked to the Father for what to do.

JUNE 9

JESUS' WILL

*And He began teaching in their
synagogues and was praised by all.*
Luke 4:15

So persuaded was Jesus of His Father's
complete love, trustworthiness and
omnipotent power over all evil that He
could relinquish His own will quickly. And
just as quickly there flowed back from the
Father the particular Word to give the
sufferer along with the necessary faith. Thus
occurred the resultant miracle healings.

JUNE 10

SELF-WILL

Seek the Lord while He may be found.
Isaiah 55:6

The words "Thou shalt have no other gods before Me" had to apply to my personal desire-world. There was nothing for it but to "put away" that most beloved of all idols inscribed "What I want." The scrapping of a treasure is always painful.

JUNE 11

SELF-WILL

He who separates himself seeks his own desire.
Proverbs 18:1

The temptation to hang onto self-will is tagged "man's autonomy" and the bait is our covetousness for understanding. It is a temptation to which I, for one, have succumbed as often as most people by always wanting to know "Why?"

SELF-WILL

*The heart of the righteous
ponders how to answer.*
Proverbs 15:28

We need to be careful not to confuse what
the old egocentric self wants – to succeed,
to get well, to be loved – with that positive,
trusting, obedient attitude that wants only
God's will for us.

TRUE DESIRE

"Do you wish to get well?"
John 5:6

How much the story of the man at the Pool of Bethesda says to me every time I read it! I thought that I yearned for healing, but in fact I was not ready to shoulder the full responsibilities of vigorous health. True prayer is dominant desire. If a person is divided he will experience emptiness and frustration.

JUNE 14

TRUE DESIRE

*(The man) had been thirty-
eight years in his sickness.*
John 5:5

There is something we can do about contradictions inside us. First, we can present our long-standing prayers to God for analysis. If there is any division of will, He will put His finger on it. Second, we can acknowledge this inner inconsistency and present it to God for healing. At this point He will almost always issue us a directive.

TRUE DESIRE

*And immediately the
man became well.*
John 5:9

The moment that we rise to obey Him,
we discover a great fact: his words *are* life
– with power to restore the atrophied will,
to quicken pallid desire, to resurrect us from
the graveclothes of a half-dead existence.

JUNE 16

OUR PATTERN

And they came to a place named Gethsemane; and He said to His disciples, "Sit here until I have prayed."
Mark 14:32

Jesus' prayer in the Garden of Gethsemane, I came to see, is the pattern for us. Christ used His free will to turn the decision over to His Father.

WISDOM

"From the tree of the knowledge of good and evil you shall not eat."
Genesis 2:17

Wisdom ... understanding – tempting bait. Except for the thoughts God chooses to share with us, it's still forbidden fruit. So long as we wear the garment of flesh, we can never understand the mind of our Creator.

JUNE 18

CHILDREN

*From the mouth of infants and nursing
babes Thou hast established strength ...*
Psalm 8:2

God uses children and grandchildren to
keep older people flexible.

JUNE 19

CHILDREN

*"I say to you, that their angels
in heaven continually behold the
face of My Father who is in heaven."*
Matthew 18:10

We are not to clutch our children to ourselves. What we hold too tightly we can drive away or break. When we give our children up to God, He will eventually give them back to us.

JUNE 20

CHILDREN

*"Whoever then humbles himself
as this child, he is the greatest
in the kingdom of heaven."*
Matthew 18:4

In the Kingdom of God the heart is tender. We grown-ups have only to watch little children to realize how calloused we have become.

JUNE 21

PRESUMPTION

Revive me according to Thy word.
Psalm 119:154

How can we tell the difference between presumption and faith? Presumption assumes something to be true in the absence of God's proof to the contrary. Faith hears and receives God's word first-hand via the Spirit speaking to our spirit, and moves forward only on that word.

JUNE 22

BAPTISM

"As for me, I baptize you in water for repentance, but He who is coming after me ... will baptize you with the Holy Spirit."
Matthew 3:11

It is as *sinners* that we receive Christ for salvation and are baptized in water. It is then as *sons and daughters* that we receive the baptism of the Spirit.

JUNE 23

THE FATHER'S WILL

*"The Son can do nothing of Himself, unless
it is something He sees the Father doing."*
John 5:19

Jesus meant it when He said that the Son
does only what He sees the Father doing.
That's altogether different from doing
something because God hasn't said not to
do it.

JUNE 24

FELLOWSHIP WITH GOD

The life that He lives, He lives to God.
Romans 6:10

Even at the moment when Christ was bowing to the possibility of an awful death by crucifixion, He never forgot either the presence or the power of God.

JUNE 25

OBEDIENCE

A tranquil heart is life to the body.
Proverbs 14:30

When we run out ahead of God, an element of daring God and of boldness bordering on impertinence, even unbelief, enters the situation. But then when we have gotten His directives and obeyed them, we no longer have to carry the responsibility for the results.

JUNE 26

OBEDIENCE

All of us like sheep have gone astray.
Isaiah 53:6

It's good to remember that not even the Master Shepherd can lead if the sheep do not follow Him but insist on running ahead of Him or taking side paths.

OBEDIENCE

"But as for me, I would seek God."
Job 5:8

Obey ... obedience ... trust ... is all over the Gospels. The pliability of an obedient heart must be complete from the set of our wills right on through to our actions.

JUNE 28

OBEDIENCE

That you may obey Jesus Christ ...
1 Peter 1:2

When we come right down to it, how can we make obedience real except as we give over our self-will in reference to each of life's episodes as it unfolds – whether we understand it or not, and even if evil appears to have initiated the episode in question?

JUNE 29

OBEDIENCE

*As obedient children, do not be
conformed to the former lusts ... but like
the Holy One who called you, be holy ...*
1 Peter 1:14-15

It should not surprise us that at the heart
of the secret of answered prayer lies the law
of relinquishment.

JUNE 30

DIVISION

You also, as living stones, are being built up as a spiritual house for a holy priesthood.
1 Peter 2:5

The God I know does not want us to divide life up into compartments – "This part is spiritual, so this is God's province, but that part over there is physical, so I'll have to handle that myself."

JULY

JULY 1

BEING BORN AGAIN

Walk in newness of life.
Romans 6:4

Our "born again" life is never our own natural life raised to its highest development. Rather, it is that life scrapped, dead, "crucified with Christ." Then to take the place of that old natural life, the Divine life condescends to its lowliest home – your heart and mine.

JULY 2

GOD'S CARE

*The Lord reigns; let
the earth rejoice.*
Psalm 97:1

If we are to believe Jesus, His Father and our Father is the God of all life and His caring and provision include a sheepherder's lost lamb, a falling sparrow, a sick child, the hunger pangs of a crowd of thousands. These vignettes say to us, "No creaturely need is outside the scope or range of prayer."

JULY 3

GOD'S SUPPLY

For the Lord is a great God,
and a great King above all gods.
Psalm 95:3

As long as we have a low threshold of expectation, we probably won't turn to God for help; our own efforts will handle it. But when we decide to be totally His person at His disposal and take on some enormous task He requires of us, then we are going to find ourselves thrown upon His unlimited supply.

JULY 4

THE INVISIBLE HAND

*In all things show yourself to
be an example of good deeds.*
Titus 2:7

It was George Washington's habit to begin and close each day with a time of prayer, alone in his room. How important this was to him is reflected in his public speeches: "No people can be bound to knowledge and adore the Invisible Hand which conducts the affairs of men more than those of the United States."

JULY 5

GOD'S POWER

*The sea is His, for it was
He who made it; and His
hands formed the dry land.*
Psalm 95:5

One of Christ's fundamental premises was
that God the Father controls all of earth's
material resources. Simple words, but what
a tremendous assertion! Most of us do not
really believe this at all. Yet the Bible
emphatically declares it.

JULY 6

GOD'S CREATION

*The earth is the Lord's,
and all it contains.*
Psalm 24:1

The magnificence of His handiwork is seen in the tumbling seas, in a sunset slashing the Grand Canyon. Ride to the top of the mountain at St. Moritz, gasp with awe at the snow-covered panorama of rugged peaks spread out at one's feet. Or see the turquoises and blues in the waters around Moorea and Bora-Bora in the South Seas.

JULY 7

GOD'S PRACTICALITY

"Declare and set forth your case."
Isaiah 45:21

Jesus would not allow those who came running after Him wailing, "Lord, have mercy," to stop there; He was forever forcing them out of this "general blessing" area by asking questions like "What do you want Me to do for you?" In other words, "Use your mind, My son. Make up your heart. God is not the Father of sloppy thinking."

JULY 8

SELF-SUFFICIENCY

(Be) imitators of those who through faith and patience inherit the promises.
Hebrews 6:12

Since God does exist, then the cult of self-sufficiency is mistaken – tragically so in some cases, misleading in all. In my case, the most spectacular answers to prayer have come following a period when I could do nothing for myself at all.

JULY 9

THE SUPREME REALITY

In (Christ) are hidden all the
treasures of wisdom and knowledge.
Colossians 2:3

So we take the first hard steps of obedience. And lo, as we stop hiding our eyes, force ourselves to walk up to the fear and look it full in the face – never forgetting that God is still the supreme reality – the fear evaporates. Drastic? Yes. But it is one sure way of releasing prayer power into human affairs.

GUIDANCE

*The prayer of the
upright is His delight.*
Proverbs 15:8

The more extensive our need, the more important it is to get God's guidance on pinpointing where and how He wants His supply to come to us. It's as if once we find the first right thread to pull, the whole of our tangled problem begins to unravel.

JULY 11

FATHERHOOD

*"(The Lord) ... will be with you. He
will not fail you or forsake you."*
Deuteronomy 31:8

We can trust the character and love of the
Father in heaven to surpass that of the best
earthly father we have ever known or can
imagine.

JULY 12

COMFORT

Strengthen the hands that are
weak and the knees that are feeble.
Hebrews 12:12

God comforts us with strength by adding
resources. His way is not to whittle down
the problem but to build up the resources.
I opened my New Testament and found
there exactly that concept of comfort.

GIVING

*Cast your bread on the
surface of the waters, for you
will find it after many days.*
Ecclesiastes 11:1

Here is an exciting principle for all those in life's holes. Of what do we have a shortage? Money? Ideas? Friends? Love? Prayer-power? Creativity? Strength? Health? Whatever it is, when we, under God's direction, give away out of our shortage, like the tide returning we get back abundance.

JULY 14

DISCIPLINE

For those whom the Lord loves He disciplines.
Hebrews 12:6

God's sternness in dealing with me did not seem quite like love. Yet I thought of the many times when it had taken far more love for me to hold my son to what I knew was right than to indulge him. This is the kind of firmness that is even a proof of love.

JULY 15

GOD'S LOVE

"HOLY, HOLY, HOLY, IS THE LORD GOD, THE ALMIGHTY."
Revelation 4:8

God's love is not dependent on our earning it. God is "for us" first, last and always. By every word and action, by all the force of His personality, Christ sought to tell us that the Father is always nearer, mightier, freer to help us than we can imagine.

JULY 16

GOD'S LOVE

*"When you pray, say: 'Father, hallowed
be Thy name. Thy kingdom come.'"*
Luke 11:2

The Gospels make it clear that to Jesus
the Father is all-loving, is of the essence of
love, cannot help loving.

JULY 17

KNOWING GOD

*At that very time He rejoiced greatly in the
Holy Spirit, and said, "I praise Thee, O
Father, Lord of heaven and earth."*
Luke 10:21

What builds trust in the Creator? Only
knowing Him so well – His motives, His
complete good will – being certain that
no pressures will make Him change,
knowing Him for a long enough time to
be sure of these things.

Discipline

It is for discipline that you endure.
Hebrews 12:7

Truth may be painful, but it makes us free. God is not interested in coddling us, but in liberating us for further creativity, for the new life that we are forced to make.

CREATIVITY

For in Him all things were created.
Colossians 1:16

The essence of creativity is to seek Him first. We begin with a seed idea or a seed talent and create something that other people need or enjoy. That plunges us directly into the stream of the Creator's unending creativity and generosity.

Negativism

I would have despaired unless I had
believed that I would see the goodness
of the Lord in the land of the living.
Psalm 27:13

All encounters in life, every personality, every institution, every relationship, is a mixture of the good and the bad. When we habitually focus on the bad, we are training ourselves in negativism.

JULY 21

NEGATIVISM

*O Lord, Thou hast brought
up my soul from Sheol.*
Psalm 30:3

In my case, I woke up twenty years into
adulthood to find myself deeply schooled
in serious negativism. That, in turn, can
bathe all of life in emotional gloom. When
the habit continues into midlife or later,
the dark glasses of criticalness can lead to
long periods of melancholy and even to
serious depression.

HABITS

*For all who are being led by the
Spirit of God, these are sons of God.*
Romans 8:14

The Holy Spirit can indeed change our
desires and our tastes and our habit
patterns. But He can't do this until we
trust Him enough to put ourselves in His
hands.

JULY 23

GOD'S PLANS

(God) is able to do exceeding abundantly beyond all that we ask or think.
Ephesians 3:20

God's plans for His children are always so much more bountiful than our best-laid plans for ourselves.

JULY 24

RICHES

*And my God shall supply all your needs
according to His riches in glory in Christ Jesus.*
Philippians 4:19

God still controls all the riches of earth
and heaven. As children of the King, we
are not to think poverty. His promise to
each of us: *If you give of yourself, your time,
your material resources to others, I will open the
windows of heaven and pour down My blessing
upon you.*

JULY 25

TRIALS

*Faith, if it has no works,
is dead, being by itself.*
James 2:17

We should not shrink from tests of our faith. Only when we are depending on God alone are we in a position to see God's help and deliverance, and thus have our faith strengthened for the next time.

THE FATHER'S REALM

*And God saw all that He had
made, and behold, it was very good.*
Genesis 1:31

To call our Father in heaven a King, in my opinion, is to understate the truth. Consider the prodigality of the Father's world. He did not create a single kind of fern, but some 10,000 kinds; not one type of palm tree but 1500 different palms.

JULY 27

GRIEF

Then Job answered the Lord, and said ... "I will ask Thee, and do Thou instruct me."
Job 42:1, 4

Trying to force oneself to be brave will not heal the heart. It is forever true that when the storms of life are savage, it is the tree that bends with the wind that survives.

GRIEF

... Martha, the sister of the deceased, said to Him, "Lord ... he has been dead four days." Jesus said to her, "Did I not say to you, if you believe, you will see the glory of God?"
John 11:39-40

Self-pity – that special illness at the heart of all grief.

UNDER THE LAW

*"I will put My law within them,
and on their heart I will write it."*
Jeremiah 31:33

In His changing of our desire-world the
Holy Spirit will deal with each of us
differently. Given that, any church or
religious group that seeks to place us back
"under law" with lists of "Thou shalt nots"
is denying the Spirit's work and interfering
with it.

JULY 30

MOTIVATION

*"For what will a man be profited, if he gains
the whole world, and forfeits his soul?"*
Matthew 16:26

When we go forth to stamp out sin, disease,
poverty, oppression – as He did – do we
keep uppermost in our minds the heart-
stirring vision of the world as God intended
it to be? Or does hatred of the enemy we
are opposing gradually fill our horizon?

JULY 31

LOVING OUR ENEMIES

"But I say to you, love your enemies."
Matthew 5:44

"Love your enemies. Do good to those who hate you ..." Here Christ was making a clear distinction between the iniquity, which he hated, and the sinner who, even though his own will was responsible for his sin, was nevertheless now the victim of it, bound by it.

AUGUST

AUGUST 1

LOVING OUR ENEMIES

*"And pray for those who persecute
you in order that you may be sons
of your Father who is in heaven."*
Matthew 5:44-45

Indeed, this command to love our enemies
is often not possible for us worldlings; it is
a miracle God Himself has to work in the
human heart.

FINANCES

*"The Lord will open for you
His good storehouse, the heavens."*
Deuteronomy 28:12

I learned that money is really only ideas that have been converted into a form usable in the exchange markets of earth. The corollary is that these ideas must be of a kind that will be of some help to other people.

AUGUST 3

FINANCES

*Then he made two sculptured
cherubim in the room of the holy of
holies and overlaid them with gold.*
2 Chronicles 3:10

The way to pray for economic resources is
to ask God for new and creative ideas that
will make a contribution – no matter how
small – to lighten the task or illumine the
lives of one's contemporaries.

AUGUST 4

THE WILL

The Lord knows the thoughts of man.
Psalm 94:11

The motivating force at the center of our physical being is our will. It is the governing power in us, the spring of all our actions. Before God we are responsible only for the set of that will – whether we decide for God's will or insist on self-will.

AUGUST 5

THE WILL

Be glad in the Lord, you righteous ones.
Psalm 97:12

Our Maker knows that our feelings are unruly, unreliable gauges. So if we see to it that our intentions (our motives) are right, we can trust God to see to the results.

UNBELIEF

*"(The Holy Spirit) will convict
the world concerning sin ... because
they do not believe in Me."*
John 16:8-9

Why does Scripture not only call unbelief
a sin, but declare it to be the fountainhead
of all sin, the sin that encompasses all other
sins? Because by our unbelief we reject
Jesus Christ, who He is, all He stands for,
what He came to earth to do.

GRUMBLING

*And the Lord spoke to Moses,
saying, "I have heard the
grumblings of the sons of Israel."*
Exodus 16:11-12

God regards even the lowest rung of
protest – complaining and grumbling –
not as a petty personality flaw, or even as
an offense against another person, but as
serious sin against Him directly.

TRUTH

And He said to them, "Follow Me."
Matthew 4:19

God wants us to use all our mind, along with our emotions and will, to love and serve Him. Therefore, we need have no fear about where Truth will lead us. He is still out ahead of the greatest scholars or scientists or theologians.

JESUS' ABILITY

*For as many as may be the promises
of God, in Him they are yes.*
2 Corinthians 1:20

Every time I reject Jesus' ability to handle
any problem or problem area of my life, I
am rejecting Him as the Lord of life.

AUGUST 10

NEEDS MET

*Therefore, since we receive a kingdom which
cannot be shaken, let us show gratitude.*
Hebrews 12:28

I realized that I need never meet any future
difficulty alone, that help from a loving
God would ever be available for the asking,
that resources beyond imagining are
always at our disposal – provided only that
we are willing to put ourselves in the
stream of God's purposes.

AUGUST 11

TESTING GUIDANCE

Thy word is a lamp to my feet ...
Psalm 119:105

The inspiration that reaches us via the unconscious should be subjected to certain tests. The writers of Scripture insist that we are open to influences not only from the Holy Spirit but also from perverse and evil spirits. Anyone who means business about God's leading will need to turn again to the Bible as a textbook.

AUGUST 12

TESTING GUIDANCE

All Thy commandments are faithful.
Psalm 119:86

God's voice will never contradict itself. That is, He will not give us a direction through the inner Voice that will ever contradict His voice in the Scriptures.

AUGUST 13

FREED FROM SIN

The Spirit of the Lord God is upon me,
because the Lord has anointed me ...
to proclaim liberty to captives ...
Isaiah 61:1

Jesus claimed to be the Savior, to be able to save us from any sin, any bondage, any problem. By disclaiming that with regard to any one of my problems, I am calling Jesus a liar and a charlatan – a fake prophet.

AUGUST 14

FREED FROM SIN

"For God did not send the Son into the world to judge the world, but that the world should be saved through Him."
John 3:17

We think of sin as the breaking of laws, whereas Jesus thinks of sin as being bound. And Jesus came to earth, He announced at the beginning of His public ministry, for the express purpose not of condemning us, but of releasing all of us sin-captives.

Freed From Sin

*If we say that we have no sin, we are deceiving
ourselves, and the truth is not in us.*
1 John 1:8

Until we see ourselves as bound in many
specific areas and in need of freeing and
saving, obviously we will have no need of
the Savior. Our danger then will be that
of approaching Jesus not as a Savior but
as a Santa Claus for the good gifts He can
give us.

Persuasion

*Therefore if any man is in
Christ, he is a new creature.*
2 Corinthians 5:17

As the printed page is increasingly peppered with four-letter words, we can't help wondering: Isn't the obscenity really our frustration at the poverty of language that no longer really communicates to people's minds and hearts? Perhaps then, the subconscious reaction goes, people can be *shocked* into paying attention.

Personal Growth

*"He who overcomes, I will grant to him
to sit down with Me on My throne."*
Revelation 3:21

My experience has been that it is only out
of a state of tension that growth can come.
It is a strange paradox that we have to be
willing to suffer the tension for a time,
knowing that it is the bridge to the next
step in our lives.

AUGUST 18

JESUS' WAY

*Then He poured water into the basin,
and began to wash the disciples' feet.*
John 13:5

The way of the cross, Jesus' way. The way
that puts others ahead of self.

PEACE OF MIND

*"Where I am, there
shall My servant also be."*
John 12:26

Peace of mind, happiness, contentment, and all their first and second cousins come to us only as by-products. The paradox is that he who tries basket weaving, not because he is fascinated by weaving, but in order to avoid his emotional problem, will end up a still-frustrated person, loathing his baskets.

RULERSHIP

*For by one Spirit we were
all baptized into one body.*
1 Corinthians 12:13

Many people are afraid of the Holy Spirit. Often unspoken is the fear, "If I assent to the Spirit, won't He then just take over and make me do all sorts of kooky things?" But from a great pool of Christian experience comes the answer. No, the Helper never violates anyone's free will.

AUGUST 21

RULERSHIP

Everlasting joy will be theirs.
Isaiah 61:7

The Holy Spirit, like each Person of the Trinity, has supreme respect for our personhood. He will never trample upon that or take us any further than we are willing to go.

THE LIGHT OF THE WORLD

Jesus spoke to them, saying,
"I am the light of the world."
John 8:12

I wonder if Christ means for us to take His "I am the light of the world" more literally than we do. Of course, the statement also points to a theological truth. But He who created the atom and the sun remains the power center, the dynamo of the physical universe.

AUGUST 23

WRITING

He who neglects discipline despises himself.
Proverbs 15:32

A person writing a book cannot wait for times of inspiration. Usually the spurts of inspired writing come as dividends from hours upon hours of grinding labor every day.

WRITING

*Get wisdom and instruction
and understanding.*
Proverbs 23:23

I discovered what many writers know, that it was well to end a day's work in the middle of a paragraph, even in the middle of a sentence. Then one's mind is forced to carry the unfinished work until the next work period, and the picking up is easier.

WRITING

*Do you see a man skilled in his
work? He will stand before kings.*
Proverbs 22:29

Clear communication in writing depends,
at least in part, on discipline. Trying to
avoid both sentimentality and diffuseness
was as exhausting as reining in a pair of
runaway horses.

AUGUST 26

PROTECTION

"Blessed is the man who trusts in the Lord ...
For he will be like a tree planted by the water
... And will not fear when the heat comes ..."
Jeremiah 17:7-8

In promise after promise, the Bible seeks
to teach us that in God and in His resources
there is physical protection surer than any
weapon or defense known to man.

ROMANCE

"He has brought me to his banquet ball,
and his banner over me is love."
Song of Songs 2:4

It was God who thought up romance in the first place. He alone, at the center of the man-woman relationship, can give to physical attraction the lustre, the idealism, the romance, the durability of which we dream.

AUGUST 28

LOVE

*"Comfort, O comfort My
people," says your God.*
Isaiah 40:1

Every human being needs love. Most of
our troubles spring from the lack of it. Like
thirsty men in a desert, we perish without
it.

JESUS' NAME

*"But for you who fear My name
the sun of righteousness will rise
with healing in its wings."*
Malachi 4:2

When we pray "in Jesus' name," we are
not simply verbalizing a word or a phrase;
rather, our petition is to the complete
character of the Lord and all of the power
implicit in His name.

JESUS' NAME

*"And you will go forth and skip
about like calves from the stall."*
Malachi 4:2

The Scripture abounds in "holy mysteries"
and the full meaning of praying in the
name of Jesus is one of those mysteries. In
heaven, the mystery is understood; on
earth we shall probably never know it fully.
Yet as we step out in faith using that name,
we do learn bit by bit.

AUGUST 31

COMMUNICATION

I thank my God in all my remembrance of you.
Philippians 1:3

Friendship and love can follow only in the wake of the heart's articulation. Mind must speak to mind; spirit to spirit.

SEPTEMBER

SEPTEMBER 1

RELIGION

*(God) ... reconciled us to Himself
through Christ, and gave us the
ministry of reconciliation.*
2 Corinthians 5:18

To some people religion is an isolated
compartment, so narrow as to be stifling.
Perhaps that is why so many flee it.

Hardness Of Heart

*Encourage one another day after
day ... lest any one of you be
hardened by the deceitfulness of sin.*
Hebrews 3:13

We are warned that toying with sin or deliberately harboring even small sins in our lives results in an accretion of the hardening process in us.

SEPTEMBER 3

FEAR

*"Therefore do not be anxious for tomorrow;
for tomorrow will care for itself."*
Matthew 6:34

"Fear not" is one of the most reiterated
exhortations in Scripture.

SEPTEMBER 4

Fear

The Lord is the defense of my life;
whom shall I dread?
Psalm 27:1

When we see fear through Jesus' eyes, it is the acting out of our disbelief in the loving Fatherliness of God. By our worrying and fretting, we are really saying, "I don't believe in any God who can help me." Thereby we are sinning against God by impugning His character and calling Him a liar.

SEPTEMBER 5

FEAR

For He Himself is our peace.
Ephesians 2:14

Behind Jesus' sharp reaction to our faithless fears lay His consistent viewpoint that this is our Father's world still in His control.

FEAR

*"As the Father gave Me
commandment, even so I do."*
John 14:31

It may seem to us at first thought that any dependence is the opposite of strength or a mature personality. But when we look closely at Jesus, we see that this is not so. Always the Master gave the impression of a moment-by-moment companionship and dialogue with the Father, yet here was a man afraid of nothing.

SEPTEMBER 7

CREATIVITY

*In the beginning God created
the heavens and the earth.*
Genesis 1:1

God, always the Creator, helps us with our creative tasks when we ask Him to. It shouldn't have surprised me to find that this meant very practical aid – in my case, help with sentence structure and transitions. All too many people still think of God as interested only in their morals and church attendance.

BELIEVERS

*He Himself bore our sins in His
body on the cross, that we might
die to sin and live to righteousness.*
1 Peter 2:24

During the Last Supper conversation Jesus
made it clear that the promises He was
making that night were not meant just for
the eleven men within the sound of His
voice, but for future believers as well. And
what He promised for the future could
scarcely be more exciting.

SEPTEMBER 9

PROBLEMS

*Here is the perseverance and
the faith of the saints.*
Revelation 13:10

When life caves in, we are to seek God in
our problem. God has a plan for every life
by which He will bring good out of evil.

SEPTEMBER 10

COMFORT

"As one whom his mother
comforts, so will I comfort you."
Isaiah 66:13

If His comfort were limited to pity or commiserating with us (as much human sympathy is), it would lead us to self-pity and that's no help at all. Rather, the Spirit's comfort puts courage into us, empowers us to cope with the strains and exigencies of life.

SEPTEMBER 11

KNOWING GOD

This hope we have as an anchor of the soul.
Hebrews 6:19

The need of all of us – whether we realize it or not – is to know whether there really is a God and, if so, to know Him in a direct and personal way through Christ. When we know Him and understand something of His love for us, then we can trust and follow Him. Only then shall we lose the pang of our heart hunger.

Revelations Of Jesus

... because He abides forever ...
Hebrews 7:24

Because the Holy Spirit is a living, always-contemporary Personality, down all the centuries there must be an ever-unfolding manifestation of Jesus, His personality, His ways of dealing with us, along with new, fresh disclosures of the mind of the Father.

HEAVEN

*After these things I looked, and behold,
a door standing open in heaven ...*
Revelation 4:1

Sometimes a person crossing the threshold between life and death gives those watching a glimpse of what lies beyond. The universal testimony in these instances is that death is nothing to be feared; that there is beauty – often rapturous music, reunion with those who have gone before, recognition, warmth and love – on the other side.

CREATIVE WRITING

*And all the sons of Israel, seeing the fire
came down and the glory of the Lord upon the
house, bowed down on the pavement with their
faces to the ground, and they worshiped.*
2 Chronicles 7:3

"No creative work," the Lord told me, "has
final impact unless it touches the reader at
the level of the emotions."

DREAMS COME TRUE

Blessed be the God and Father of our
Lord Jesus Christ, who has blessed us.
Ephesians 1:3

There is no limit to what the combination of dreams and prayer can achieve. I have seen amazing results in many areas — like finding the right mate or the right job, or locating the ideal house, or rearing children, or building a business.

DREAMS COME TRUE

But as for me, my prayer
is to Thee, O Lord.
Psalm 69:13

Before handing your dream over to God, ask yourself these questions: Will my dream fulfill my needs and talents? Does my dream take anything or any person belonging to someone else? Am I willing to make all my relationships right? Do I want this dream with my whole heart? Am I willing to wait patiently for God's timing?

DREAMS COME TRUE

Seek the Lord while he may be found.
Isaiah 55:6

As for the danger that our dreams may spring from our selfish human will rather than God's will, there are tests for this. Only when a dream has passed such a series of tests – so that we are certain that our heart's desire is also God's dream *before* we pray – can we pray with faith and thus with power.

DREAMS COME TRUE

Now may the God of hope fill you
with all joy and peace in believing.
Romans 15:13

There seem to be periods when the heart's desire is like a seed planted in the dark earth and left there to geminate. This is not a time of passiveness on our part. There are things we can and must do – fertilizing, watering, weeding – hard work and self-discipline. But the growth of that seed is God's part of the process.

DREAMS COME TRUE

*... being fully assured that what He had
promised, He was able also to perform.*
Romans 4:21

Long before we see the fruition of our
hopes, in fact the very moment a God-
given dream is planted in our hearts, a
strange happiness flows into us. I have
come to think that at that moment all the
resources of the universe are released to help
us. Our praying is then at one with the
will of God.

A Special Work

Bless the Lord, you His angels,
mighty in strength, who perform His word.
Psalm 103:20

We should never hesitate to try the impossible. God does have a special work for us to do in the world. Should this involve a big dream, we must believe that the bigger the dream, and the more loving and unselfish it is, the greater will be God's blessing on it.

THE PERFECT BALANCE

*For the kingdom of God is ... righteousness
and peace and joy in the Holy Spirit.*
Romans 14:17

In the Holy Spirit we have the perfect
balance of God's love – infinite tenderness
on the one side, infinite strength on the
other.

SEPTEMBER 22

INTELLECT VS. FAITH

Whatever a man sows, this he will also reap.
Galatians 6:7

Our virtual deification of human intellect goes straight back to Thomas Aquinas (1227-1274) who taught that while man's will fell from grace, his intellect did not. Whenever anyone sets up his reasoning against God's, he is going the Aquinas way of humanistic autonomy, even though he may piously call it faith.

SEPTEMBER 23

IMMORTALITY

*"Everyone who lives and believes in
Me shall never die. Do you believe this?"*
John 11:26

Not only did Jesus tell us about immortality, but to prove it He rose from the dead and over a period of forty days appeared and reappeared to more than five hundred witnesses.

TRUE WISDOM

"Unless a grain of wheat falls into the earth and dies, it remains by itself alone."
John 12:24

The only true wisdom is facing up to what we actually are – creatures – and then yielding ourselves to the wisdom of our Creator. This yielding is relinquishment. And as we relinquish our own defective human judgment, it feels like death because it *is* death – the beginning of the end of the old Adam in us.

WAITING

The Lord is good to those who wait for Him.
Lamentations 3:25

The Lord seems constantly to use waiting as a tool for bringing us the very best of His gifts.

SEPTEMBER 26

WAITING

*"For you will go out with joy ... Instead of
the thorn bush the cypress will come up."*
Isaiah 55:12-13

Waiting itself, if practiced according to
biblical patterns, seems to be a strange but
dynamic kind of communication between
man and God. It is God's oft-repeated way
of teaching us that His power is real and
that He can answer our prayers without
interference and manipulation from us.

WAITING

And in the shadow of
Thy wings I sing for joy.
Psalm 63:7

When we leave our prayers with the Father, we find for ourselves what the saints and mystics affirm, that during the dark waiting period when self-effort ceases, a spurt of astonishing spiritual growth takes place in us. Afterward we have qualities like more patience, more ability to hear His voice, greater willingness to obey.

WAITING

*Wait for the Lord; be strong, and
let your heart take courage.*
Psalm 27:14

Waiting seems to be a kind of acted-out prayer that is required more often and honored more often that I could understand until I saw what remarkable faith-muscles this act develops.

SEPTEMBER 29

WAITING

Weeping may last for the night,
but a shout of joy comes in the morning.
Psalm 30:5

The Bible extols waiting, partly because it requires qualities that the Lord wants to encourage in us, like patience. But there is another reason too. Waiting works. It is a joining of man and God to achieve an end, and the end is always a form of the Easter story.

Waiting

Those who wait for the Lord,
they will inherit the land.
Psalm 37:9

Jesus had a great deal to say about His Father's timing, the principle that there is a God-given sequence and rate of growth for everything in His Creation – "First the blade, and then the ear."

OCTOBER

OCTOBER 1

ROUGH TIMES

*When he falls, he shall not be
hurled headlong; Because the Lord
is the One who holds his hand.*
Psalm 37:24

You and I are living in rough times. We must make our way through minefields of evil, booby traps of deception, brush fires of sickness, wastelands of economic disaster, burning deserts of disappointment. "I won't take you out of this world," Jesus told us. "But don't be afraid, because I've overcome that world of dangers."

PRAYER

*One of His disciples said to
Him, "Lord, teach us to pray."*
Luke 11:1

God has dared to arrange it so that He is actually dependent upon us in the sense of our prayers being necessary and all important to the carrying out of His will on earth.

OCTOBER 3

PRAYER

*Delight yourself in the Lord; and He
will give you the desires of your heart.*
Psalm 37:4

As we recognize our ignorance about praying aright and our helplessness, and actively seek the Spirit's help, our prayer life becomes the anteroom to amazing adventures.

OCTOBER 4

GOD'S TIMING

*The steps of a man are
established by the Lord;
and He delights in his way.*
Psalm 37:23

I remember once being in a situation where the Lord told me to stand silently by, saying nothing, even though I thought I knew the answer to a problem. Even within this smaller scope I was to wait on His timing, His invisible action in another human heart. It was an astounding experience in poised expectancy.

OCTOBER 5

SELF-SUFFICIENCY

Bless the Lord, O my soul,
And forget none of His benefits.
Psalm 103:2

We are helpless without the God who made us and whose Spirit animates us. Yet the cult of self-sufficiency is not yet dead. It beats daily at our eardrums. It encourages selfishness. It devaluates working for the joy of working instead of for the reward of money; it scorns living to serve other people.

OCTOBER 6

SELF-SUFFICIENCY

*Remember His wonders which
He has done, His marvels, and
the judgments uttered by His mouth.*
Psalm 105:5

Happiness flees when self takes the center
of the stage.

PRAYER

*How precious also are Thy thoughts to
me, O God! How vast is the sum of them!*
Psalm 139:17

Mysteries about prayer are always ahead
of knowledge – luring, beckoning on to
further experimentation.

OCTOBER 8

IDOLATRY

Do not be idolaters.
1 Corinthians 10:7

Idealizing can soon become idolizing, and no human being should idolize another. We open ourselves to inevitable disillusionment when we do. And we do the object of our idolizing an injustice, for pedestal-sitting can be a lonely business.

OCTOBER 9

UNDERSTANDING

*"I have loved you with
an everlasting love."*
Jeremiah 31:3

Was Jesus teaching us how to use the law
of relinquishment when He said, "Resist
not evil"? Stop fleeing from and denying
this terrible prospect. Look squarely at the
possibility of what you fear most. "Obey
Me," He says. "Then – after that – you
will know and begin to understand."

OCTOBER 10

THE NEED FOR PRAYER

(May) ... the Father of glory ... give
to you a spirit of wisdom and of
revelation in the knowledge of Him.
Ephesians 1:17

All around us are those caught in bondages, imprisoned in fears, hampered by disease to whom Jesus longs to bring His release and His joy. But He waits on *our* prayers. It's a solemn thought.

OCTOBER 11

VISUALIZING

*I pray that the eyes of your
heart may be enlightened.*
Ephesians 1:18

It's because everything starts with an idea
that dreaming, visualizing, is important.
In fact it can be a way of prayer — a very
effective way.

OCTOBER 12

LONELINESS

*Walk by the Spirit, and you will
not carry out the desire of the flesh.*
Galatians 5:16

Since God made us for companionship,
loneliness is not His plan for us. But there
is a price to be paid in seeking God's
remedy. This includes a decision to give
up self-pity, the determination not to
compromise honor, and the willingness to
let Him fill our heart with His love, which
can then spill out into loving concern for
others.

Knowing

*(Give) ... thanks to the Father, who
has qualified us to share in the
inheritance of the saints in light.*
Colossians 1:12

In some situations the Good Shepherd
leads us from relinquishment on into
knowing. Such knowing is different from
trying to think positively or making
affirmations. It is not our doing at all; it is
the gift of God.

OCTOBER 14

GOD'S DESIRES

*"Your Father knows what you
need, before you ask Him."*
Matthew 6:8

God's dreams are usually more wonderful
than ours. The problem for most of us is
how to stretch ourselves enough to accept
His munificence.

OCTOBER 15

RELINQUISHMENT

*Humble yourselves, therefore, under
the mighty hand of God, that He
may exalt you at the proper time.*
1 Peter 5:6

Even while it hopes, our relinquishment
must be the real thing – and this giving
up of self-will is the hardest thing we
human beings are ever called on to do.

OCTOBER 16

RELINQUISHMENT

For by these He has granted to us
His precious and magnificent promises.
2 Peter 1:4

Whenever a loving Father grants our wish, the Word appears in exterior circumstances and the miracle happens – we understand that relinquishment and faith are not contradictory.

OCTOBER 17

GOD'S IDENTITY

"Father, glorify Thy name."
John 12:28

I realized how often we attribute emotions and deeds to God that we would ascribe only to the most depraved of human minds. Probably no personality in the universe is so maligned as that of the Creator.

OCTOBER 18

GOD'S IDENTITY

*Jesus said to him, "... He who has
seen Me has seen the Father ..."*
John 14:9

When we persist in mistaken and tragic
ideas of the Creator, how can God show
us what He is really like? He solved this
problem in the Incarnation.

JOY

You also became imitators of us and of the Lord, having received the word in much tribulation with the joy of the Holy Spirit.
1 Thessalonians 1:6

The promise is not that the Christian will have only joyous circumstances, but that the Holy Spirit will give us the supernatural gift of joy in whatever circumstances we have.

JOY

*About midnight Paul and Silas were
praying and singing hymns of praise to
God, and the prisoners were listening to them.*
Acts 16:25

Those other prisoners must have been
listening with incredulity to Paul and Silas,
for there is nothing natural about singing
and praising while one's feet are chained
in stocks. Obviously, genuine joy in such
circumstances is impossible for us humans;
it is clearly supernatural.

TRUSTING JESUS

"Lo, I am with you always."
Matthew 28:20

As we pray in faith, our hands are still in His. Our hearts are still obedient. But now he has led us out of the frightening darkness, with only the pressure of His hand to reassure us, into the sunlight. All along our hearts told us so. Relinquishment? Faith? Just daring to trust Jesus.

Praying In Secret

*But He Himself would often slip
away to the wilderness and pray.*
Luke 5:16

How Jesus loved to pray in secret Himself!
He had a habit of rising up a great while
before day and going outdoors – to a
mountainside or some other deserted place
– to pray. Perhaps because of the small,
crowded Palestinian houses, that was the
only way He could find privacy and
solitude.

Praying In Secret

(Jesus) ... went off to the mountain to pray, and He spent the whole night in prayer to God.
Luke 6:12

Before major decisions – such as His choosing of the twelve apostles – Jesus would pray alone an entire night. And going back to the beginning of His public ministry, we find Jesus going off into the desert for forty days and nights of seclusion and concentrated prayer. He knew that power was needed; in secret He would find it.

Praying In Secret

"God is spirit; and those who worship Him must worship in spirit and truth."
John 4:24

There are other reasons why Jesus instructs us to pray in secret. Real power in prayer flows only when man's spirit touches God's Spirit. As in worship, so in prayer.

PRAYING IN SECRET

I meditate on Thee in the night watches.
Psalm 63:6

Transparent honesty before Him is easier for us in isolation.

THE HOME

Ascribe to the Lord, O families of the peoples,
ascribe to the Lord glory and strength.
Psalm 96:7

Husbands and wives are basically incompatible. Parents are incompatible with their children. God made us all different. That's why the home is His classroom for molding and shaping us into mature people.

OCTOBER 27

RELEASE FROM BONDAGE

*"These things I have spoken to you,
that My joy may be in you ..."*
John 15:11

Jesus spent His days going about looking into pain-filled eyes and in summary fashion — with delight — releasing men and women from the enemy's bondages. These were joyous tasks because the Lord of life loathed sickness and disease and broken relationships and insanity and death. So day by day He left behind a string of victories.

God's Character

*"How much more shall your
Father who is in heaven give what
is good to those who ask Him!"*
Matthew 7:11

Jesus acted as if there was never any question of the Father's willingness to supply all needs. Divine love delighted in dispelling pain, in restoring sanity, in straightening crooked limbs and opening blind eyes, even in banishing premature death.

THE INNER RESERVOIR

*"When therefore you give alms,
do not sound a trumpet before you."*
Matthew 6:2

Jesus told us that if we want to become fulfilled and productive persons, we must reverse the usual process. That is, we are to divest ourselves of weaknesses, faults and sins by confessing them openly, while kindnesses and good deeds are to be kept secret. The result is an inner reservoir of power.

OCTOBER 30

CONFESSION

*If we confess our sins, He is faithful
and righteous to forgive us our sins and
to cleanse us from all unrighteousness.*
1 John 1:9

Facing up to ourselves in confession is the-
rapeutic, provided we move on to forgiveness and do not wallow in our wrongdoing.

JOY IN TRIALS

"I have overcome the world."
John 16:33

Certainly Jesus was aware of life's problems and disappointments: "In the world you have tribulation," He promised His disciples. "But," he added, "take courage; I have overcome the world." Or in other words, "Cheer up! The worst that the world can do is no match for Me."

NOVEMBER

NOVEMBER 1

JESUS' JOY

*(God) ... has anointed Thee with
the oil of joy above Thy fellows.*
Psalm 45:7

"Thou hast loved righteousness, and hated
wickedness; therefore God, Thy God, has
anointed Thee with the oil of joy above
Thy fellows." He who knew no sin and *is*
righteousness had a personality sparkling
and overflowing with a degree of gladness
that none of us can match. How could it
be otherwise!

FORGIVENESS

"If you do not forgive men, then your Father
will not forgive your transgressions."
Matthew 6:15

I became aware of a compartment in my being in which I had locked certain persons whom I disliked. They could go their way; I would go mine. But now Christ seemed to be standing by the locked door saying, "That isn't forgiveness. It won't do. No closed doors are allowed. The Kingdom of God is the kingdom of right relationships."

TRUST

Surely our griefs He Himself bore ...
Isaiah 53:4

When anyone of us has a painful experience that the mind cannot equate with a loving God, there is this remedy: "I want You and Your presence, Lord, even more than I want understanding. I choose You." When we ask this, He then gives peace and illumination as His gift.

NOVEMBER 4

In Residence

In Thy presence is fullness of joy.
Psalm 16:11

Queen Elizabeth's standard flying over Buckingham Palace in London is the sign that the queen is in residence. Joy looking out of the Christian's eyes is the sign that the King is in residence within.

MANAGEMENT

As for me, I shall behold
Thy face in righteousness.
Psalm 17:15

The keys and the management of my "house" had to be turned over to Christ. For how could I ask Him to heal me until He was completely in charge?

NOVEMBER 6

JOY

Serve the Lord with gladness;
come before Him with joyful singing.
Psalm 100:2

Joy is a sure sign of the King's approval.

HEARING GOD

*He made known to us the mystery of His
will ... with a view to an administration
suitable to the fullness of the times.*
Ephesians 1:9-10

Seeking the substantiating of divine facts
to my natural mind means that I go to
Jesus and ask, "Lord, speak to me about
this. What do You want to tell me about
it? Let me see this situation through Your
eyes."

NOVEMBER 8

DIFFICULT PEOPLE

"Bless those who curse you."
Luke 6:28

As soon as we begin to obey Him, we find that blessing those with whom we are having difficulties and the *answer* to these difficulties go hand in hand.

DIFFICULT PEOPLE

*"... for He causes His sun to rise
on the evil and the good ..."*
Matthew 5:45

If you and I were running the world, probably we would not allow the wicked to prosper. But the simple truth is that Jesus was and always is the Realist. He simply took it for granted that because God is all love, the wicked *will* often prosper.

DIFFICULT PEOPLE

*"For if you love those who love
you, what reward have you?"*
Matthew 5:46

"**I**f you are going to be true children of
your Father in heaven," said Jesus, "then
pray for the very best to happen to
everyone you know – no matter how they
may have hurt you." Is He saying that
wickedness is of no consequence to God?
Not at all! The point is that accusing
prayers do not change people. Only joyous
love redeems.

DIFFICULT PEOPLE

"The joy of the Lord is your strength."
Nehemiah 8:10

We can love our "enemy" enough to ask gladness for him, only if He who was anointed with so much gladness does it for us.

DIFFICULT PEOPLE

Keep yourselves in the love of God.
Jude 21

Now obviously we cannot bless and pray for people who despitefully use others or with whom we are at odds unless we recognize that no self-effort can manage this and let Christ – living in us – love others for us.

DIFFICULT PEOPLE

*"He who believes in Him
shall not be disappointed."*
1 Peter 2:6

Praying blessings on an "enemy" is not a
risky way to pray, once we see that God's
way is to make "His sun to rise on the just
and on the unjust," and that His sun of
joy is the only power in the universe capable
of transforming hearts – no matter what
their problems.

NOVEMBER 14

Entering In

"Ask, and you will receive,
that your joy may be made full."
John 16:24

Growing up in a believing family is not to be undervalued. It is still the ideal beginning, because it is the foundation of the happiest possible childhood. Yet I know now that something more is needed: each human being must enter into Life for himself. There is no such thing as inheriting Christianity.

NOVEMBER 15

ENTERING IN

Clothe yourselves with humility.
1 Peter 5:5

Let's not mistake it: Entering into a direct Father-child relationship does take childlikeness. The door through which we enter into Life is a low door. And sometimes it is the humble and the needy who can show the rest of us the way.

NOVEMBER 16

REVELATION

By revelation there was made
known to me the mystery.
Ephesians 3:3

When we realize the range of important questions that will always elude the net of final intellectual or scientific proof, then we begin to appreciate the significance of revelation. Surely here is a most important gift we should ask for more often.

JESUS' LOVE

The love of God has been poured out within
our hearts through the Holy Spirit.
Romans 5:5

Perhaps the greatest distance any of us ever
has to travel is that long trek between the
head and the heart. Just so, the love of Jesus
is something that I must *experience*, and
only the Holy Spirit can make me feel that
great, tender love.

NOVEMBER 18

INTERVENTION

*"(God) ... does great and unsearchable
things, wonders without number."*
Job 5:9

I think it a mistake to think of God's
intervention only in terms of great events
and dramatic circumstances – a sudden
healing, or the saving of a life in jeopardy.
After all, most of our days are full of
ordinary events and common experiences.
Are we to believe that God has no interest
in these?

NOVEMBER 19

CLAIMING HIS RICHES

You do not have because you do not ask.
James 4:2

The riches of grace must be claimed. The process goes like this: God has made a promise. If there are conditions attached to it, we do our best to meet them. We make an act of claiming this promise at a specific time and place. God fulfills the promise in His own time and His own way.

THE BIBLE

With Thy counsel Thou wilt guide me.
Psalm 73:24

We have to study the Bible intelligently, not as if the Scriptures were a sort of holy rabbit's foot, but for its wisdom in the broad sweep of its teaching about the nature of God and of man.

NOVEMBER 21

HEALING PRAYER

My times are in Thy hand.
Psalm 31:15

Many authentic healings through prayer are a gradual process rather than a one-time miracle. The complete healing thus takes time and persistently repeated prayer work. And this slower timing, by the way, is consistent with all normal processes of the body, as well as of everything in nature.

NOVEMBER 22

HEALING PRAYER

*"And I say to you, ask, and
it shall be given to you."*
Luke 11:9

The joyous news is that we do not need to
wait for the special mission of the healing
evangelist. God wants all His people to
believe in His good will of health and to
step out and experiment in prayer. He
wants to use all of us.

NOVEMBER 23

HEALING PRAYER

*"... because of his persistence he will get
up and give him as much as he needs."*
Luke 11:8

I wonder now why I ever expected five or
ten minutes of prayer to cure everything.
Or why any of us has accepted the principle
often taught that to pray more than once
for a healing betrays a lack of faith. The
Lord taught the opposite. And in two
separate parable-stories on prayer He com-
mends dogged perseverance.

PRAYER

*For God is not a God of
confusion but of peace.*
1 Corinthians 14:33

The purpose of all prayer is to find God's will and to make that will our prayer, so that as Jesus bade us pray in the Lord's Prayer, the Father's will may be done as perfectly on earth as it is in heaven.

NOVEMBER 25

PRAYER

*If we ask anything according
to His will, He hears us.*
1 John 5:14

If there are any conditions attached to a promise we receive from God, we do our best to meet them, for He who will not let us down also will not let us off. To illustrate: The condition of having our sins cleansed is our forgiveness of others; the condition of material blessing is that we give priority to the Kingdom of God.

Inner Judgment

*In all your ways acknowledge Him,
and He will make your paths straight.*
Proverbs 3:6

In relation to the matter of inner judgment, the Quakers were fond of saying, "Mind the checks." They meant that when we feel a strong doubt that a particular course is right, then wait. Don't move on it. Or to put it positively, we should always move forward in faith – never out of fear.

In A Storm

*As they were sailing along (Jesus) ...
fell asleep; and a fierce gale of wind de-
scended upon the lake, and they began to
be swamped ... And they ... woke Him up.*
Luke 8:23-24

The peace that Jesus gives us through the
Comforter is not dependent on any outside
circumstances. It is given right in the midst
of great activity or stress or trouble or grief
while the storm rages all around us.

NOVEMBER 28

IN A STORM

(Jesus) ... rebuked the wind and the surging waves, and they stopped, and it became calm.
Luke 8:24

I was also, minute by minute, learning something else – that our God can handle even the worst that can happen to us as finite human beings. Since Christ is beside us, no troubles that life can bring need cast us adrift. This is a knowledge that can release us from lifelong bondage to fear.

HEARING GOD

*Martha was distracted
with all her preparations.*
Luke 10:40

I wonder whether God does not try more often than we know to save His children from the accidents and disasters of our lives on this earth. But many of us do not practice the art of listening to the inner Voice with regard to small everyday matters. Because we are not tuned in, He cannot get His message through to us even in emergencies.

NOVEMBER 30

HEARING GOD

(God) ... gives perseverance
and encouragement ...
Romans 15:5

If a strong inner suggestion is from God,
it will strengthen with the passing of time.
If it is not from Him, in a few days or
weeks it will fade or disappear entirely.

DECEMBER

DECEMBER 1

THE NEXT WORLD

*And ... the living creatures give glory and
honor and thanks to Him who sits on the
throne, to Him who lives forever and ever.*
Revelation 4:9

Our world is connected with joy and hope
to another; we who refuse to explore its
spiritual and physical boundaries with zest
and a sense of adventure, who will not lift
our eyes to its far horizons, cheat only
ourselves.

DECEMBER 2

MIRACLES

Power belongs to God.
Psalm 62:11

"Power belongs to God." Jesus believed this so totally that over and over He moved out to stake His life and His entire reputation on the validity of this fact.

DECEMBER 3

MIRACLES

*"All authority has been given
to Me in heaven and on earth."*
Matthew 28:18

Jesus knew perfectly well about natural law — seedtime and harvest, disease and death. All this made not one whit of difference to Him. Very simply, Jesus' faith was that His Father was over and above all natural law; He was omnipotent over anything in earth or in heaven.

DECEMBER 4

MIRACLES

He who did not spare His own Son, but
delivered Him up for us all, how will He not
also with Him freely give us all things?
Romans 8:32

The disciples' acceptance of Jesus' bodily resurrection changed their viewpoint about everything. In the face of this stupendous miracle-fact, any other miracle was possible and probable. Then God could do *anything*. Believing that, they were prepared to let the Spirit use them to stand the Roman world on its head.

DECEMBER 5

GOOD AND EVIL

*In all these things we overwhelmingly
conquer through Him who loved us.*
Romans 8:37

A good, hard look at evil as it is presented
in the Bible and an obedient following
through of the whole story left me with
one overwhelming impression – a great
feeling of confidence and victory.

DECEMBER 6

GOOD AND EVIL

*And the seventy returned with
joy, saying, "Lord, even the demons
are subject to us in Your name."*
Luke 10:17

The Bible story of the conflict between
good and evil is not downbeat at all, but
upbeat; it is the story of the total defeat of
evil because of the absolute power of Christ.

DECEMBER 7

GOOD AND EVIL

Do not give the devil an opportunity.
Ephesians 4:27

I remember our quoting at one another one of Hannah Smith's favorite maxims: "All discouragement is of the devil." Of course the remedy is to realize the source to the depression and to remind oneself that spiritual reality can never be gauged by feelings.

STEPS OF FAITH

The testing of your faith produces endurance.
James 1:3

Those saints who have had the most experience here tell us that God uses our most stumbling, faltering faith-step as the open door to His doing for us "more than we ask or think."

DECEMBER 9

INTERCESSION

*"If two of you agree on earth about
anything that they may ask, it shall
be done for them by My Father."*
Matthew 18:19

The Bible insists that we have to ask for
God's help in order to get it. That is the
point of petitionary prayer. And the asking
seems to have more power when many join
their petitions in agreement.

DECEMBER 10

FAULTS

Never take your own revenge.
Romans 12:19

Continually, we need to beware of our incorrigible human blindness to our own faults as contrasted with the way we see other people's faults as if under a giant magnifying glass.

DECEMBER 11

FORGIVENESS

But Jesus was saying, "Father, forgive them ..."
Luke 23:34

At the heart of the Christian Gospel lies forgiveness, the greatest miracle of all.

DECEMBER 12

FORGIVENESS

"And forgive us ... as we also have forgiven."
Matthew 6:12

Forgiveness has two sides that are inseparably joined: the forgiveness each of us needs from God, and the forgiveness we owe to other human beings. Most of us prefer not to face up to the fact that God's forgiveness and man's are forever linked.

DECEMBER 13

FORGIVENESS

Be kind to one another.
Ephesians 4:32

Every one of us is guilty before God. There are sins of the mind and the spirit as well as of the body. Yet God is willing freely to forgive us, no matter what we have done, *provided* we are willing to "be kind one to another, tenderhearted, forgiving each other."

DECEMBER 14

FAITH FIRST

Jesus, the author and perfecter of faith ...
Hebrews 12:2

Until science can finally prove life after death beyond evidential experiences, we are backed up against faith. For anything relating to the spirit, the irreversible order is faith first, then knowledge. That is because faith has a way of slicing through prejudicial and intellectual barriers and opening the eyes of the spirit.

DECEMBER 15

FAITH FIRST

He who comes to God must believe ... that
He is a rewarder of those who seek Him.
Hebrews 11:6

In Jesus' ministry of healing the spirit, the mind and the body, faith seems to have been necessary before the divine act, not (as logic would have it) afterward.

DECEMBER 16

TRIALS

(God) ... delivered us from the domain of darkness, and transferred us to the kingdom of His beloved Son.
Colossians 1:13

Paul learned that God allows us to have disappointments because He wants us to see that our joy is not in worldly pleasures. Our joy is in the fact that we have a relationship with God. Few of us ever understand that message until circumstances have divested us of any possibility of help except by God Himself.

Unbelief

*Now the Lord is the Spirit; and where the
Spirit of the Lord is, there is liberty.*
2 Corinthians 3:17

The truth is that none of us can go anywhere in the Christian life so long as we are chained with unbelief. For until we believe that Jesus is the Savior of our life, for whatever our problem is, there is nothing He can do for us.

UNITY

*And the congregation of those who
believed were of one heart and soul.*
Acts 4:32

The passion of Jesus' heart for oneness will
be fulfilled – but only by the Helper's work
in our world. After all, this oneness is of
man's inner spirit, and only the Spirit can
melt our hard hearts and our stubborn
insistence that we are right and everyone
else wrong.

UNITY

We, who are many, are one body in Christ,
and individually members one of another.
Romans 12:5

Scripture continually insists on the principle of our connectedness as a fact of human
life: "We (are) members one of another."

DECEMBER 20

LISTENING

*"Take My yoke upon you,
and learn from Me."*
Matthew 11:29

Is it possible for an opinionated woman in
her autumn years to become like a child
and sit at the feet of Jesus with one idea –
to hear what He will say?

DECEMBER 21

FEAR

"Do not be afraid, little flock ..."
Luke 12:32

Knowing that all people struggle with fear, Jesus often prefaced what He was about to say to His fellow humans with the words "Fear not." Therefore my prayer is, "Lord, I hand my fears over to You, fears of all kinds."

HABITS

*"I will put My law within them,
... and I will be their God."*
Jeremiah 31:33

I see now how God helps us change long-standing habits. What happens is that our tastes begin to change. Something that we liked a lot suddenly is not so appealing. When we understand that it is the Lord Himself working, then we can stop resisting our own changing tastes, thank Him and flow with the new direction of the tide.

DECEMBER 23

SURRENDERED

*He laid down His life for us; and we ought
to lay down our lives for the brethren.*
1 John 3:16

No wonder we can do no mighty works until the surrender to Jesus is complete. Until He has been allowed to come and make His home in me – letting all self go – I will be praying for others, doing His work, in my name and in my nature rather than in His.

The Door To Hope

Blessed is he who trusts in the Lord.
Proverbs 16:20

There is a crucial difference between acceptance and resignation. Resignation lies down in the dust of a godless universe and steels itself for the worst. Acceptance says, "I'll look unblinkingly at my situation. But I'll also open my hands to accept willingly whatever a loving Father sends." Acceptance never slams the door on hope.

DECEMBER 25

GREATER WORKS

*For the gifts and the calling
of God are irrevocable.*
Romans 11:29

Was Jesus seriously promising that we —
you and I — would not only do these same
works, but even *greater* works? Could He
be serious? We find that His early apostles
did take this preposterous promise at face
value and proceeded to act upon it.

DEPENDING ON GOD

*"Now they have come to know that everything
Thou hast given Me is from Thee."*
John 17:7

Jesus' helplessness meant a total dependence upon His Father for everything.

THE HOLY SPIRIT

*"I will ask the Father, and He
will give you another Helper."*
John 14:16

The Holy Spirit is a Person – one of the
three Persons of the Godhead. As such, He
possesses all the attributes of personality.
He has a mind; He has knowledge; He has
a will.

DECEMBER 28

THE HOLY SPIRIT

"He abides with you, and will be in you."
John 14:17

The Spirit, being a Person, is a Friend whom we can come to know and to love. One of His most lovable characteristics is that He deliberately submerges Himself in Jesus; He works at being inconspicuous.

DECEMBER 29

THE HOLY SPIRIT

The Lord God will cause righteousness and
praise to spring up before all the nations.
Isaiah 61:11

As our willingness and receptivity increase,
we will also experience repeated fillings of
the Holy Spirit. These will come as we step
out in ministry. Special filling and special
outpouring will be given for situations we
alone could never handle. This has been
the experience of many individuals across
the centuries.

DECEMBER 30

THE HOLY SPIRIT

And your ears will hear a word behind
you, "This is the way, walk in it."
Isaiah 30:21

Jesus' promise to you and me is that the
Helper will be with us always, day and
night, standing by for any protection we
need and for every emergency. Our only
part is to reconize His presence and to call
upon Him in joyous faith.

DECEMBER 31

THE HOLY SPIRIT

"It is to your advantage that I go away; for if I do not go away, the Helper shall not come to you."
John 16:7

We wonder how anything could be more wonderful than the physical presence of our Lord. Yet Jesus never spoke lightly or thoughtlessly. And here we have His solemn word in His Last Supper talk with His apostles that there *is* something better – His presence in the form of the Holy Spirit.